T0242262

Communications in Computer and Information Science   **1213**

Commenced Publication in 2007
Founding and Former Series Editors:
Simone Diniz Junqueira Barbosa, Phoebe Chen, Alfredo Cuzzocrea,
Xiaoyong Du, Orhun Kara, Ting Liu, Krishna M. Sivalingam,
Dominik Ślęzak, Takashi Washio, Xiaokang Yang, and Junsong Yuan

Editorial Board Members

More information about this series at http://www.springer.com/series/7899

Suresh Balusamy · Alexander N. Dudin ·
Manuel Graña · A. Kaja Mohideen ·
N. K. Sreelaja · B. Malar (Eds.)

Computational Intelligence, Cyber Security and Computational Models

Models and Techniques for Intelligent Systems and Automation

4th International Conference, ICC3 2019
Coimbatore, India, December 19–21, 2019
Revised Selected Papers

Springer

Editors
Suresh Balusamy
PSG College of Technology
Coimbatore, India

Alexander N. Dudin ⓘ
Belarusian State University
Minsk, Belarus

Manuel Graña
University of the Basque Country
Leioa, Spain

A. Kaja Mohideen
PSG College of Technology
Coimbatore, India

N. K. Sreelaja
PSG College of Technology
Coimbatore, India

B. Malar
PSG College of Technology
Coimbatore, India

ISSN 1865-0929   ISSN 1865-0937   (electronic)
Communications in Computer and Information Science
ISBN 978-981-15-9699-5   ISBN 978-981-15-9700-8   (eBook)
https://doi.org/10.1007/978-981-15-9700-8

This Springer imprint is published by the registered company Springer Nature Singapore Pte Ltd.
The registered company address is: 152 Beach Road, #21-01/04 Gateway East, Singapore 189721, Singapore

Preface

The contemporary growth in the dynamic realms of software, hardware, and networking leads to abundant scope in research and development of computer science and its thrust areas. To provide a broad spectrum of interdisciplinary research forum, a biennial International Conference on Computational Intelligence, Cyber Security, and Computational Models (ICC3 2019) was organized by the Department of Applied Mathematics and Computational Sciences of PSG College of Technology, India, during December 19–21, 2019.

The key objective of this conference is to cover the state-of-the-art scientific approaches, technologies, tools, case studies, and findings to explore the cutting-edge ideas and to promote collaborative research in the areas of computational intelligence, cyber security, and computational models to enable establishing research relations worldwide under the theme of "Contemporary Models and Applications for Computational Paradigms."

Computational intelligence encompasses a broad set of techniques such as neural networks, fuzzy systems, evolutionary computation, and nature-inspired computational methodologies to address complex real-world problems. This track aims to bring out novel techniques for computation and visualization, find solutions for computationally expensive problems, and explore data within them, be it classification, clustering, or feature engineering.

The increasing use of the internet and social media has made cyber security more important. Cyber security is of paramount importance for government organizations and is a vital asset to the nation. Growing cyber threats such as data theft, phishing scams, and other cyber vulnerabilities demand that users remain vigilant about protecting their data. The cyber security track in this conference aims to bring together researchers, practitioners, developers, and users to explore cutting-edge ideas and end results.

Computational models are mathematical models that are simulated using computation to study complex systems from the effects of drugs on the body to the interactions of nations in the global economy. This conference provides a window to the novel endeavors of the research communities by publishing their works and highlighting the value of computational modeling as a research tool when investigating complex systems. This track aims at fostering research interactions in all aspects of computational science and engineering, and focuses on developing computational models needed to meet the demands of computer systems users, while exploring the new potential of computation engines.

There has been an increase in submissions to ICC3 2019 over the past few editions. This year, we received 37 papers in total, and accepted 9 papers (24.32% percent). Each submitted paper went through a rigorous review process.

We would like to express our sincere gratitude to all the keynote speakers, International Advisory Committee, authors, Program Committee, and reviewers for their invaluable contributions to the success of this conference. We also extend our warmest gratitude to Springer for their continued support in publishing the ICC3 proceedings on time and in excellent production quality. The partial support from the sponsors Cognizant Technologies, Council of Scientific and Industrial Research, 24[7], and Defense Research and Development Organization (DRDO) is acknowledged.

Being a strong and stimulating event towards a diligent and interdisciplinary research amidst scholars, we hope this tradition will continue in the future. The next ICC3 conference will be held at PSG College of Technology, India, in 2021.

September 2020   Suresh Balusamy
                                                       Alexander N. Dudin
                                                          Manuel Graña
                                                      A. Kaja Mohideen
                                                        N. K. Sreelaja
                                                            B. Malar

Organization

Chief Patron

L. Gopalakrishnan   PSG & Sons Charities Trust, India

Patron

K. Prakasan   PSG College of Technology, India

Organizing Chair

R. Nadarajan   PSG College of Technology, India

Program Chair

Suresh Balusamy   PSG College of Technology, India

Computational Intelligence Track Chair

Kaja Mohideen A.   PSG College of Technology, India

Cyber Security Track Chair

Sreelaja N. K.   PSG College of Technology, India

Computational Models Track Chair

Malar B.   PSG College of Technology, India

Advisory Committee Members

Anitha R.	PSG College of Technology, India
Sai Sundara Krishnan G.	PSG College of Technology, India
Lekshmi R. S.	PSG College of Technology, India
Senthil Kumar M.	PSG College of Technology, India
Geetha N.	PSG College of Technology, India
Bella Bose	Oregon State University, USA
Alexander Rumyantsev	Petrozavodsk State University, Russia
Rein Nobel	Vrije University, The Netherlands

Contents

Computational Models

Computational Intelligence

Comparing Community Detection Methods in Brain Functional Connectivity Networks

Reddy Rani Vangimalla⑩ and Jaya Sreevalsan-Nair$^{(\boxtimes)}$⑩

Graphics-Visualization-Computing Lab, E-Health Research Center,
International Institute of Information Technology - Bangalore,
26/C, Electronics City, Bangalore 560100, India
reddyrani.vangimalla@iiitb.org, jnair@iiitb.ac.in

Abstract. Brain functional networks are essential for understanding the functional connectome. Computing the temporal dependencies between the regions of brain activities from the functional magnetic resonance imaging (fMRI) gives us the functional connectivity between the regions. The pairwise connectivities in matrix form correspond to the functional network (fNet), also referred to as a functional connectivity network (FCN). We start with analyzing a correlation matrix, which is an adjacency matrix of the FCN. In this work, we perform a case study of comparison of different analytical approaches in finding node-communities of the brain network. We use five different methods of community detection, out of which two methods are implemented on the network after filtering out the edges with weight below a predetermined threshold. We additionally compute and observe the following characteristics of the outcomes: (i) *modularity* of the communities, (ii) symmetrical node-partition between the left and right hemispheres of the brain, i.e., *hemispheric symmetry*, and (iii) *hierarchical modular organization*. Our contribution is in identifying an appropriate test bed for comparison of outcomes of approaches using different semantics, such as network science, information theory, multivariate analysis, and data mining.

Keywords: Brain functional connectivity · Network analysis · Node-community · Community detection · Factor analysis · Infomap · Louvain community detection · Hierarchical clustering

1 Introduction

Understanding the connectivities between different regions in the brain has been a challenge in the area of brain network analysis. Non-invasive and in-vivo imaging techniques are commonly used for brain studies today, attributed to the advances in neuroimaging domain. fMRI is one of the widely used brain imaging modalities. Similarly, other modalities such as electroencephalography (EEG) and magnetoencephalography (MEG) techniques are also used to create func-

© Springer Nature Singapore Pte Ltd. 2020
S. Balusamy et al. (Eds.): ICC3 2019, CCIS 1213, pp. 3–17, 2020.
https://doi.org/10.1007/978-981-15-9700-8_1

tional networks (fNet) to analyze the brain activities. The nodes of these networks correspond to regions of interest (ROIs) in the brain confirming to a specific anatomical atlas, e.g., Automated Anatomical Labeling atlas (AAL) [38], Dosenbach atlas (DOS) [12]. The edges between the nodes are computed based on the relationships between all these regions of the brain, which encode the connectivity between the nodes[1]. Here, we focus on the pairwise correlation between nodes in networks computed from fMRI at resting state. For example, the sample network datasets with Brainnet Viewer [41] are computed as correlation matrices. Functional connectivity is inferred from the correlation of the blood-oxygenation level dependent (BOLD) signals of fMRI imaging [28,39] between nodes, as defined for the brain network [37].

In the conventional workflow of brain functional connectivity network (FCN) analysis [13,22,40], these connectivity matrices[2] are subjected to sparsification by retaining only edge weights of these networks, which are greater than a threshold value. These sparsified matrices are either used directly as weighted graphs or binarized to give unweighted graphs. These preprocessed networks are referred to as *edge-filtered networks*.

Community[3] detection is one of the frequently implemented analysis of FCN. Sporns [36] has discussed about modularity being used for functional segregation and integration, for finding communities and hubs. Functional segregation is the process of identification of ROIs that are related with respect to their neuronal process and are represented as a module. These modules in the network are also referred to as communities, where they have dense intra-community links and sparse inter-community links. Sporns has discussed how functional segregation has been done using multiple approaches, two of which include performing the conventional community detection in the network, and identification of "Resting State Networks" (RSNs), respectively. An RSN is a set of regions in the brain, which show coherent fluctuations of the BOLD signal. Bullmore et al. [6] have described how graph-based methods can be used on brain FCN, and explained the clustering tendency and modular community structure of the brain. In this work, we systematically compare different community detection procedures using an appropriate case study, which is a test bed.

As a complex network with small-world behavior, brain FCN exhibits the property of dense edge connections between nodes of the community and sparse connections across the communities [2]. Meunier *et al.* [24] have discussed how the brain networks, like any other complex networks, have multiple topological scales and hence hierarchical node-groupings, along with modularity. Meunier *et al.* [24] have also explained the existence of both overlapping and non-overlapping communities that display hierarchical modularity. In this work, we

---

[1] Connectivity matrices of functional networks could be computed using several methods [13], e.g., correlation, mutual information, phase coherence.

[2] Connectivity matrix of a **network** corresponds to the adjacency matrix of the **graph**.

[3] We use the terms *community*, *module*, *cluster*, and *node-partition* interchangeably in this paper.

focus on non-overlapping node-partitions, *i.e.*, each node belongs to only one module/community. Here, we study the modular behavior of nodes and the hierarchical organization of these modules.

In the edge-filtered networks, network science approaches are strongly influenced by the threshold value used for filtering edges. Since the network topology itself changes drastically depending on the choice of the threshold, the choice has to be carefully made. Jeub *et al.* [18] have used a range of threshold values and a consensus method for clustering the nodes in a completely connected network. Lancichinetti *et al.* [21] have explained the reasons to consider different values of thresholds to get different edge-filtered networks, and then use the consensus of the outcomes from these networks to determine the clusters of a complex network. It is also known that applying a single threshold value on network tends to discard weak and/or negative-signed edges, whose relevance has not been considered [13]. At the same time, finding a threshold interval is also a difficult problem [13]. Given the essential role of edge filtering in FCN analysis, we evaluate its role in community detection by comparing the outcomes using the completely connected brain FCN[4], *i.e.* without applying a threshold, against the edge-filtered variants of the same network, in a suitable test bed.

Our Contributions: We compare different functional segregation methodologies on the FCN. The edge-filtered networks reveal the topology of the significant subnetwork(s). However, applying a threshold on the network may not preserve the semantics of the entire network, which calls for independently studying the complete network. We compare the results derived from both edge-filtered and complete networks to evaluate an ideal node partitioning of the given FCN. The crucial questions we address here are:

– How do the chosen approaches implemented on the complete network compare to those on it's edge-filtered variant?
– Do the different functional segregation methods (tend to) converge at n node-partitions, *i.e.*, is there a value of n for which the node partitionings tend to be identical?
– If such a number n exist, then what is it's biological significance?
– In different functional segregation methodologies, how can we study the hierarchical organization of the node partitions?

Frequently used notations: Functional Connectivity Network (FCN), Louvain Method (LM), Infomap (IM), Exploratory Factor Analysis (EFA), Hierarchical Clustering (h-clust), Hierarchical Consensus Clustering (HC), Automated Anatomical Labeling atlas (AAL), ground truth (GT).

2   Methods

Our objective is to find the modules in the brain network with maximum modularity, with a preference for methods which extract hierarchical organization

---

[4] We refer to these networks as the *complete network*.

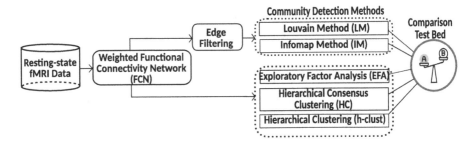

Fig. 1. Our proposed workflow for using a test bed for comparing different node partitioning techniques in the human functional connectivity network.

within the modules. There are several state-of-the-art approaches for fulfilling this objective. Our gap analysis shows that a systematic comparison of these methods with differences in preprocessing the network is essential to understand the salient aspects of these methods. We select five methods with different underlying principles and where not all use edge filtering, and propose a case study to compare them. Our workflow is given in Fig. 1.

Network Construction: The FCN is generated using fMRI data from multiple subjects in a cohort. First, an FCN is computed per subject, and the network connects different ROIs, which are the parcellations of the entire brain using a specific atlas, e.g., AAL. The mean time courses (BOLD signal) of the ROIs are extracted, and Pearson's correlation coefficients are computed between the nodes. Further, Fisher's r-to-z transformation is applied, thus giving z-score matrices, which are then aggregated across different subjects to get a single unweighted matrix. Thus, the FCN corresponding to this matrix is a completely connected graph, with the ROIs as nodes and the correlation between them as edge weights. In our work, the choice of the dataset is further restricted by the requirement of positive semi-definiteness of the matrix, so as to make it eligible for exploratory factor analysis (EFA).

Edge Filtering: Upon filtering out the edges with weights below an appropriate cutoff value [13], the FCN has been shown to exhibit small-world characteristics [22]. Small-world networks have clustering property, which enables finding communities using the modularity measure [14]. Hence, filtering edges is one of the popularly used preprocessing methods in FCN analysis. The threshold for edge filtering is selected by observing a value at which the network changes topology. This change can be identified by analysing statistical properties of the edge weights and their distribution, or by studying the network properties after applying discrete values of threshold, such as node degree distribution (Fig. 2(i)) and percolation analysis (Fig. 2(ii)).

However, applying edge filtering is fraught with stability issues, *i.e.*, slight perturbations in the threshold cause observable changes in the network topology at different threshold values (Fig. 2(iii)). The circular layout places the nodes in circles, which correspond to communities. We observe that the network filtered using different thresholds show different topology, and hence different modular organization. The circular layout, which can be stacked horizontally or vertically, is flexible in showing the instability in network depending on the choice of threshold.

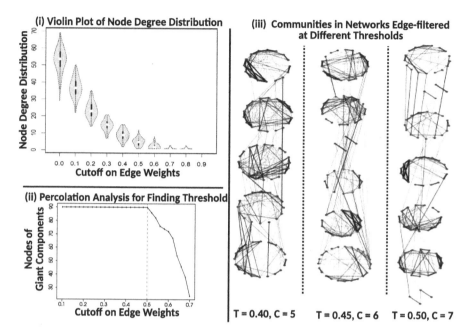

Fig. 2. Case study analysis: (i). The violin plot shows the degree distribution of the nodes of the network at different thresholds on edge values, and the elbow curve here is used for finding the optimal threshold for edge-filtering. (ii). The plot of size of giant components (#nodes) at each threshold of edge weights, using percolation analysis [5] is used for finding cutoff. (iii). The networks with edges filtered using different thresholds 'T' show different topologies, as shown by their graph layout using the stacked circular layout of nodes in their communities 'C' extracted using Louvain community detection. The edge width is proportional to the correlation value. The plot is generated using Cytoscape, utilizing group attribute layout.

Node Partitioning: Here, we focus on different node-partitioning methods with non-overlapping communities, which is known as hard clustering. Our objective is to compare five such methods using an appropriate test bed. We use two community detection methods on the edge-filtered network, namely, Louvain community detection (LM) [4] and Infomap (IM) [31]. The remaining three methods, which use the entire correlation matrix, *i.e.*, the complete network, include exploratory factor analysis (EFA) [15], hierarchical clustering (h-clust) [19], and hierarchical consensus clustering (HC) [18]. For the methods used in edge-filtered networks, graph-based techniques automatically provide the number of clusters, which can be used in methods expecting them as inputs.

LM and IM are graph-based methods used for community detection on the sparsified network. LM is a greedy optimization method that maximizes the modularity of the network using an iterative method. Every node is initially considered to be a community, and communities are merged using the nearest neighbor criterion when the modularity value Q is computed. The algorithm is iterated until all nodes are grouped with possible maximum modularity value. An information-theoretic method, IM is one of the fastest and accurate methods for identifying communities [27] and is widely used in understanding modules in FCN. It is based on the principle that there is a higher likelihood of a random walker most taking steps within a dense community than across communities. The community detection methods LM and IM, essentially exploit the network topology to find appropriate *cuts* in the network to identify densely connected subnetworks. Thus, the methods that are used on edge-filtered network are semantically different from those using the complete network, such as EFA, h-clust, and HC.

EFA is known to be an exploratory or experimental method used for correlation analysis, which uses maximum likelihood function [9] to find *factors*. The factors determine a causal model based on which the correlations between the random variables, *i.e.*, nodes in the FCN here, can be explained. Thus, a factor is an entity to which a group of nodes belong to, and we consider a set of factors as a node partitioning, modules, or communities, here. h-clust, implemented using different linkage methods, is a clustering technique used in data mining to extract hierarchical clusters. We choose to use h-clust owing to the known structure of hierarchical modularity of the brain FCN [24]. We have experimented with single, complete, average, and ward linkage methods in h-clust. HC method has been exclusively used on brain networks, where the clusters are identified using generalized Louvain community detection [20] method with fixed resolution value ($\gamma = 1$). The clusterings are aggregated using consensus. Here, we implement HC with 100 clusters and $\alpha = 0.1$ [17], where the parameter α decides if co-clustering of two nodes is by chance or by their clustering tendency.

Modularity: We choose to use the modularity metric, Q, to measure the effectiveness of node-partitions from each method. The most widely used Newman-Girvan modularity measure [14,26] is used on both directed and undirected networks, where Q measures the difference between the fraction of intra-community edges and the expected fraction of such edges based on node degrees. Q is in the range $[-1, 1]$, where positive values indicate clarity in partitioning. As a first-cut, we do not consider the resolution parameter here.

$$Q = \frac{1}{2m} \sum_{C \in P} \sum_{i,j \in C} \left[A_{ij} - \frac{k_i k_j}{2m} \right], \text{ and } k_i = \sum_{\substack{j=1 j \neq i}}^{j \leq N} A_{ij}, \tag{1}$$

where A_{ij} is the edge weight between nodes i and j, k_i and k_j are degrees of the nodes in the network consisting of N vertices, m edges, and C communities.

Comparison Test Bed: We propose appropriate settings for comparing the five chosen methods, as there are fundamental differences in the semantics of the methods. We need to ensure that the outcomes are generated with certain fixed settings so that a comparison of the outcomes is scientifically valid. The edge-filtered network used for LM and IM is ensured to be the same. Even though LM and IM automatically give the number of communities, the numbers vary owing to the differences in the methodologies. In EFA, the number of factors n_f is an input. We take the interval we have obtained from n_p in LM and IM for n_f, so that we can compare the outcomes of EFA with those of LM and IM. For h-clust and HC, since we can use an interval of n_p required for different hierarchical levels, we use the same interval as used for EFA.

Comparative Analysis: We use Q for quantitative, and Sankey diagrams for qualitative comparisons. The latter has been used as alluvial diagrams [32] for studying changes in compositions of modules in networks. We additionally perform ground truth analysis, both quantitatively and qualitatively.

3   Experiments and Results

We use a specific case study to build the test bed for comparison. We choose a FCN dataset for which we have identified ground truth in literature. We then prepare the edge-filtered variant of the chosen FCN by selecting threshold using different methods. After performing node partitioning using the chosen five methods (Sect. 2), we perform a comparative analysis of their outcomes.

Test Bed – Dataset and Ground Truth: We have used the FCN dataset published along with BrainNet Viewer [41], which is generated using the AAL atlas. There are 90 nodes in the FCN. The edge weights are the correlations computed from the resting-state fMRI data of 198 subjects in the Beijing Normal University, provided in the 1000 Functional Connectome Project [3], of healthy right-handed volunteers in the age group of 18–26 years and of which 122 are female. The fMRI scanning was performed in the eyes-closed (EC) state of subjects in state of wakefulness. The network is generated after removing data of one subject owing to rotation error. The test bed requires a ground truth (GT) for this specific dataset, for which we use the findings on a similar dataset used by He *et al.* [16]. Even though the fMRI data in our case study and that identified as GT are different, the demographics of the subjects involved and the processing done on the two datasets are the same. Hence, we take the result of five functional modules by He *et al.* [16] to be the GT, *i.e.* the reference communities. The module identification for the GT has been done using simulated annealing approach, thus, avoiding *similarity bias* with any of our chosen methods.

Community Detection in FCN: We have compared the communities of the network obtained using five different methods, i.e., LM, IM, EFA, h-clust, and HC, after preparing the test bed (Sect. 2). We compute an edge-filtered variant of the FCN by identifying an appropriate threshold using the inferences from elbow graph for degree distribution at each threshold (Fig. 2(i)) and using percolation analysis (Fig. 2(ii)). In our case study, we get optimal thresholds as $T = 0.4$

and $T = 0.5$, respectively. At $T = 0.5$, we observe the disintegration of a giant connected component in the network (Fig. 2(ii)). When $T > 0.5$, in Fig. 2(i), we observe that the node degree distribution is uniform, and the network exhibits uniform topology rather than communities. Overall, at $T = 0.4$, we observe more stability in the dataset; hence, we have chosen $T = 0.4$, as the optimal threshold for the edge-filtered variant to be used in LM. We have also verified against the binarized edge-filtered variant of the network that has been published [41], the threshold used is $T = 0.4$.

We have also run experiments with threshold $T \in [0.4, 0.5]$ to study the change in topology (Fig. 2(iii)). We have observed that for $T = \{0.4, 0.45, 0.5\}$, we get $\{5, 6, 7\}$ communities using LM, and $\{7, 9, 12\}$ using IM, respectively. In our case study, IM leads to over-segmentation. We have also observed that for $T > 0.6$ the community detection of the network using LM does not include all the 90 nodes. We have used the number of partitions as a criterion for comparing outcomes of community detection between two different methods, in addition to the strict criterion of $T \in [0.4, 0.5]$, in our test bed. Thus, we have compared results of LM using $T = 0.4$ with those of EFA using $n_f = 5$, and similarly those of IM using $T = 0.45$ with those of EFA using $n_f = 9$, given that the optimal value is determined using parallel analysis.

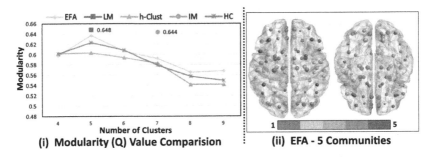

(i) Modularity (Q) Value Comparision   **(ii) EFA - 5 Communities**

Fig. 3. (i). Modularity (Q) values of node partitioning for LM, IM, EFA, h-clust with average linkage, and HC with $\alpha = 0.1$, show trends for hierarchical modules, and high values for LM and IM. (ii). Hemispheric symmetry of nodes or ROIs is observed in the visualization of modules in FCN using brain-surface visualization [41] (BNV), implemented using MATLAB.

The methods on complete networks, namely EFA, h-clust, and HC, require the number of modules as input to give outputs to be compared with those of LM and IM. The optimal value of n_f for EFA is computed using a scree plot [7] and parallel analysis. In our case study, $n_f = 9$ is the optimal number of factors according to the parallel analysis scree plot. However, we have empirically chosen $n_f = 5$, given that modularity score is highest for this value, and also, this is equivalent to the GT. Figure 3(i) shows us that for all the methods, the highest Q value is observed when the network has five modules, which confirms with the GT. For $n_p = 5$, LM shows the maximum Q, which can be attributed to its greedy characteristic. At five modules, EFA performs at par with LM. We have used R packages for implementing node partitioning, [1,10,11,30,34], and Cytoscape [33] for graph layout.

We have used the BrainNet viewer [41] for visualizing the node-communities on the brain surface (Fig. 3(ii)) in the spatial context. The axial view of the brain shows *modular organization spatially, i.e.,* neighboring nodes are grouped in a module and *hemispheric symmetry* of the nodes. Hemispheric symmetry implies that both left and right hemispherical nodes of the same brain region tend to co-cluster. EFA with $n_f = 5$, LM on the network with edge-filtering at threshold $T = 0.4$, and GT demonstrate similar modules, but with modular organization and hemispheric symmetry. We have additionally implemented each of our proposed approaches, independently as ensemble runs, *i.e.* implemented multiple times with slight changes in parameters, *e.g.,* n_f for EFA, and tree-cut for h-clust and HC. Our motivation is to compare hierarchical modular organization in FCN.

Comparative Analysis: The Sankey plot [29] or alluvial diagram [32] effectively demonstrates a qualitative comparison of the composition of communities. Figure 4(i) demonstrates that at $np = nf = 5$, outputs of LM and EFA are similar, as 83 out of 90 nodes were grouped similarly in both the methods. At $n_p = n_f = 5$, LM and EFA have the highest modularity value Q. The edge crossings in (Fig. 4(i)) between LM and EFA are due to one node in the AF4[5] cluster, and six nodes in the AF5 cluster in EFA. We observe a similar degree of mismatch between EFA with h-clust, at $n_f = n_p = 5$. However, unlike the mismatch with LM, the community sizes in h-clust are not uniformly distributed as in EFA and LM. In h-clust, we use the consensus of the node-groupings with different linkage methods of hierarchical clustering, namely single, complete, average, and ward. The tree-cut is the deciding parameter for n_p, and hierarchy is guaranteed with all linkage methods, by design. The matching is at 86.67%, *i.e.,* 12 out of 90 nodes showed grouping different from EFA. Except for the cluster AH2, the other clusters in h-clust have inconsistent mappings with EFA (Fig. 4(i)). When compared to single, complete, average, and ward linkage methods of h-clust, the average-linkage method exhibited the highest matching percentage with EFA.

Interestingly, we have observed that implementing IM on the network with edges filtered at threshold $T = 0.45$ gives nine communities, and the optimal $n_f = 9$ for EFA, as per the parallel analysis scree plot. Hence, as discussed earlier, in our test bed, we compare the outcomes between IM ($T = 0.45$) and EFA ($n_f = 9$). We observe more edge crossings between IM and EFA, indicating that the node-groupings failed to display similar correspondence (Fig. 4(ii)). But, interestingly, we observe lesser edge crossings between EFA ($n_f = 5$) and EFA ($n_f = 9$)

---

[5] In Fig. 4, 5, and 6, the communities are named in the format XY where X is {A, B, C, D}, which corresponds to {5, 6, 7, 9} node-communities, and the value of Y is {L, I, F, H, HC, He}, which corresponds to {LM, IM, EFA, h-clust, HC, GT}, respectively. For example, **AL4** represents the fourth community out of five communities ($A = 5$) identified using the method LM (L).

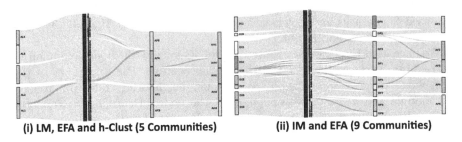

| **(i) LM, EFA and h-Clust (5 Communities)** | **(ii) IM and EFA (9 Communities)** |

Fig. 4. The composition of node-communities from multiple methods is compared using Sankey plot, where the middle vertical bar (in blue) corresponds to the node-IDs, and LM and IM are computed on the edge-filtered network at a threshold T. (i). Comparison of LM at $T = 0.4$, EFA at $n_f = 5$, and h-clust at $n_p = 5$ (average linkage) LM and EFA shows more similarity of composition and sizes of communities than LM and h-clust. (ii). Comparison of IM with $T = 0.45$, EFA with $n_f = 9$, and EFA with $n_f = 5$ show differences between IM and EFA, including fragmentation in IM. The naming convention of the communities is given in the footnote[5]. (Color figure online)

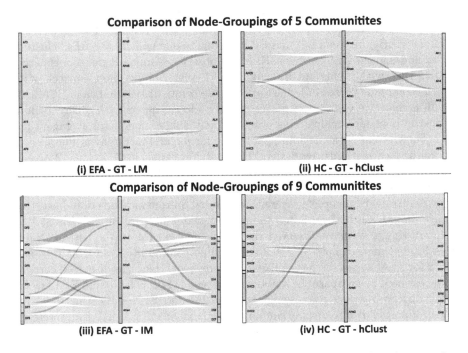

Comparison of Node-Groupings of 5 Communitites

| **(i) EFA - GT - LM** | **(ii) HC - GT - hClust** |

Comparison of Node-Groupings of 9 Communitites

| **(iii) EFA - GT - IM** | **(iv) HC - GT - hClust** |

Fig. 5. Comparative visualization of mapping of nodes between our selected approaches and ground truth (GT) in [16]. Comparison against GT of (i). EFA ($n_f = 5$) and LM ($T = 0.4$), (ii). h-clust and HC, at $n_p = 5$, (iii). EFA ($n_f = 9$) and IM ($T = 0.45$), (iv). HC and h-Clust at $n_p = 9$. The naming convention of the communities is given in the footnote[5].

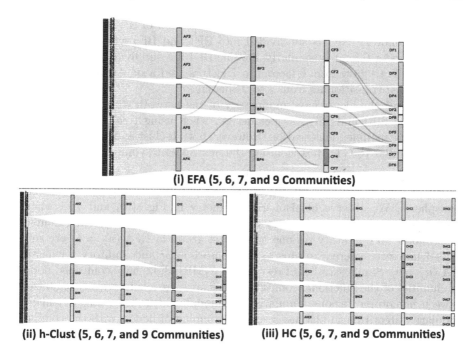

(i) EFA (5, 6, 7, and 9 Communities)

(ii) h-Clust (5, 6, 7, and 9 Communities)   **(iii) HC (5, 6, 7, and 9 Communities)**

Fig. 6. Visualizing the hierarchical modularity from five to nine modules using a cascading effect in a Sankey plot with communities identified using (i). EFA, (ii). h-clust, and (iii). HC. The naming convention of the communities is given in the footnote[5].

modules Fig. 6(i)). This observation is due to the revelation of the characteristic of hierarchical modularity in the FCN when progressively increasing n_f in EFA.

When comparing against GT [16] using Sankey diagrams as in Fig. 5(i) to (iv), we observe that the edge-crossings and inconsistent node-groupings are less in the case of EFA, and more in the case of h-clust. The matching of results with GT is 90.00%, 88.89%, 85.56%, and 83.34%, for EFA, LM, HC, and h-clust, respectively. We observe that the edge crossings are least in the case of EFA-GT-LM, for $n_f = n_p = 5$ (Fig. 5(i)) and HC-GT-h-clust, for $n_p = 9$ (Fig. 5(iv)), indicating similar grouping. But when we closely observe in the latter, the size distribution of the communities in HC-GT-h-clust does not match.

Overall, we conclude that when $n_f = n_p = 5$, EFA and LM, with $T = 0.4$, behave similar to each other, and also with GT. Additionally, EFA exhibits hierarchical modularity in our case study.

Hierarchical Modularity: We know that h-clust and HC show hierarchy in their community detection or clustering owing to the design of preserving hierarchy by performing divisive hierarchical clustering. However, we observe the same in EFA, when we increase or decrease n_f within the range [5, 9]. From Fig. 5, we have observed how EFAconfirms with the GT, and now we observe the hierarchical characteristic. Thus, in this case study, we observe that outcomes of

EFA demonstrates a hierarchical modular organization of the functional brain. In Fig. 6(i), module AF1 is subdivided into BF1 and BF6 when transitioning from 5 factors or 6 factros; similarly, module BF4 has subdivided into modules, CF4 and CF7, to grow from 6 factors to 7 factors, and a similar pattern can be observed when transitioning from 7 to 9 clusters.

We observe the hierarchical modularity of the network when using h-clust, and HC (Fig. 6(ii) and (iii)), as per design, when using tree-cut for deciding parameter for module identification. However, both h-clust and HC failed to get outcomes similar to GT, thus violating the hemispheric symmetry of modules.

Discussions: Our analysis gives results similar to that of Mezer *et al.* [25], where node communities exhibited *symmetric* patterns between left and right hemispheres. We observe hemispheric symmetry in Fig. 3(ii), and 4(i), where EFA showed both better symmetry and hierarchical modularity. For example, sensorimotor and auditory regions of the first group in EFA ($n_f = 5$) are sub-divided into two different groups as the sensorimotor and auditory regions in EFA ($n_f = 6$). Similar studies of resting-state fMRI [8, 42] have confirmed node-communities of the functional connectivity network are symmetrically organized between homotopic regions. Similarly, the modules identified using Newman's modularity algorithm in [23] has a similar grouping of nodes, with the communities we got from LM and EFA. The regions, hippocampus, and thalamus of sensorimotor system, have always exhibited symmetric patterns between the left and right hemispheres and are consistently clustered together in the same group for all values of n_p and n_f.

The biological significance of these five modules is that they correspond to largest functional modules known to exist in the brain [24] as well as the resting state networks usually extracted from fMRI data [35]. The five modules are known to be medial occipital, lateral occipital, central, parieto-frontal and fronto-temporal systems [24].

Such comparisons would not have been possible without establishing our proposed test bed. We have demonstrated that an appropriately designed test bed enables comparison of outcomes of module identification across different methodologies governed by different semantics. There are shortcomings in our methodology related to: (i) identification of thresholds for edge filtering, as well as (ii) comparing properties of the methodologies. While identifying thresholds, specific discrete values, *i.e.* $\{0.4, 0.45, 0.5\}$, were considered which could have missed values in the intervals. A better idea would be to use ranking of edge weights in the network to eliminate one edge at a time, and then analysing the network. In this work, we have not compared the robustness of our chosen methods and properties related to reproducibility [16].

4 Conclusions

In this work, we have compared five different approaches for community detection of functional connectivity network. Firstly, using edge-filtering for topological analysis of functional brain networks, we have chosen node-community detection as an outcome of our proposed workflow. In lines of node-community detection, we have proposed the use of graph-based Louvain and information-theoretic based Infomap methods on edge-filtered weighted networks. Secondly, we have introduced matrix-based exploratory factor analysis, distance-based hierarchical clustering and hierarchical consensus clustering for node-community detection, based on the semantics of the connectivity matrices. Using our proposed test bed, we can now answer the question: "For the chosen approaches and an appropriate set of parameters for implementing them, does a number, n, exist for a specific FCN, such that the node partitionings tend to be identical?". We have found it to be **five** in our case study.

Our work demonstrates how a test bed can be used for systematic comparison of community detection methods in FCN. We have also shown how an explorative correlation-analysis method, such as EFA, can be used for community detection. We observe that both Louvain community detection and EFA perform equivalently when extracting the optimal number of communities on the network. EFA additionally showcases hierarchical organization, when changing n_f progressively. We have found that the biological significance of our results as the five largest functional modules of the brain. Thus, overall, in our case study, EFA performs well in ground truth analysis, and characteristics of hemispheric symmetry of nodes in FCN and hierarchical organization. In the context of newer trends in the functional connectivity studies, our study on resting-state data can be extended to specific cognitive task-based studies. Our study is valuable as a first step towards identifying a test bed for the comparative analysis of node-partitioning in FCNs across networks with different pre-processing steps.

Acknowledgments. This work has been supported by the Visvesvaraya Ph.D. Scheme for Electronics and IT, Ministry of Electronics and Information Technology, Government of India.

References

1. Adler, D.: vioplot: Violin plot. R package version 0.2 (2005). http://CRAN.R-project.org/package=vioplot
2. Bassett, D.S., Bullmore, E.: Small-world brain networks. Neurosci. **12**(6), 512–523 (2006)
3. Biswal, B.B., et al.: Toward discovery science of human brain function. Proc. Natl. Acad. Sci. **107**(10), 4734–4739 (2010)
4. Blondel, V.D., Guillaume, J.L., Lambiotte, R., Lefebvre, E.: Fast unfolding of communities in large networks. J. Stat. Mech. Theory Exp. **2008**(10), P10008 (2008)
5. Bordier, C., Nicolini, C., Bifone, A.: Graph analysis and modularity of brain functional connectivity networks: searching for the optimal threshold. Front. Neurosci. **11**, 441 (2017)
6. Bullmore, E., Sporns, O.: Complex brain networks: graph theoretical analysis of structural and functional systems. Nat. Rev. Neurosci. **10**(3), 186 (2009)
7. Cattell, R.B.: The scree test for the number of factors. Multivar. Behav. Res. **1**(2), 245–276 (1966)

8. Chen, G.: Modular reorganization of brain resting state networks and its independent validation in Alzheimer's disease patients. Front. Hum. Neurosci. **7**, 456 (2013)
9. Costello, A.B., Osborne, J.W.: Best practices in exploratory factor analysis: four recommendations for getting the most from your analysis. Pract. Assess. Res. Eval. **10**(7), 1–9 (2005)
10. Couture-Beil, A.: rjson: Json for r. R package version 0.2 **13** (2013)
11. Csardi, G., Nepusz, T.: The igraph software package for complex network research. Int. J. Complex Syst. **1695**(5), 1–9 (2006)
12. Dosenbach, N.U., et al.: Prediction of individual brain maturity using fMRI. Science **329**(5997), 1358–1361 (2010)
13. Fallani, F.D.V., Richiardi, J., Chavez, M., Achard, S.: Graph analysis of functional brain networks: practical issues in translational neuroscience. Phil. Trans. R. Soc. B **369**(1653), 20130521 (2014)
14. Girvan, M., Newman, M.E.: Community structure in social and biological networks. Proc. Natl. Acad. Sci. **99**(12), 7821–7826 (2002)
15. Harman, H.H.: Modern Factor Analysis. University of Chicago Press, Chicago (1976)
16. He, Y., et al.: Uncovering intrinsic modular organization of spontaneous brain activity in humans. PloS ONE **4**(4), e5226 (2009)
17. Jeub, L.G., Sporns, O., Fortunato, S.: Hierarchical Consensus clustering implemented in MATLAB (2018). https://github.com/LJeub/HierarchicalConsensus
18. Jeub, L.G., Sporns, O., Fortunato, S.: Multiresolution consensus clustering in networks. Sci. Rep. **8**(1), 3259 (2018)
19. Johnson, S.C.: Hierarchical clustering schemes. Psychometrika **32**(3), 241–254 (1967)
20. Jutla, I.S., Jeub, L.G., Mucha, P.J.: A generalized Louvain method for community detection implemented in MATLAB (2011). http://netwiki.amath.unc.edu/GenLouvain
21. Lancichinetti, A., Fortunato, S.: Consensus clustering in complex networks. Sci. Rep. **2**, 336 (2012)
22. Langer, N., Pedroni, A., Jäncke, L.: The problem of thresholding in small-world network analysis. PLoS ONE **8**(1), e53199 (2013)
23. Liao, W., et al.: Small-world directed networks in the human brain: multivariate granger causality analysis of resting-state fMRI. Neuroimage **54**(4), 2683–2694 (2011)
24. Meunier, D., Lambiotte, R., Fornito, A., Ersche, K., Bullmore, E.T.: Hierarchical modularity in human brain functional networks. Front. Neuroinform. **3**, 37 (2009)
25. Mezer, A., Yovel, Y., Pasternak, O., Gorfine, T., Assaf, Y.: Cluster analysis of resting-state fMRI time series. Neuroimage **45**(4), 1117–1125 (2009)
26. Newman, M.E., Girvan, M.: Finding and evaluating community structure in networks. Phys. Rev. E **69**(2), 026113 (2004)
27. Orman, G., Labatut, V., Cherifi, H.: On accuracy of community structure discovery algorithms. J. Converg. Inf. Technol. **6**(11), 283–292 (2011)
28. Park, H.J., Friston, K.: Structural and functional brain networks: from connections to cognition. Science **342**(6158), 1238411 (2013)
29. Reda, K., Tantipathananandh, C., Johnson, A., Leigh, J., Berger-Wolf, T.: Visualizing the evolution of community structures in dynamic social networks. Comput. Graph. Forum **30**(3), 1061–1070 (2011)
30. Revelle, W.R.: psych: Procedures for personality and psychological research (2017)

31. Rosvall, M., Bergstrom, C.T.: Maps of random walks on complex networks reveal community structure. Proc. Natl. Acad. Sci. **105**(4), 1118–1123 (2008)
32. Rosvall, M., Bergstrom, C.T.: Mapping change in large networks. PloS ONE **5**(1), e8694 (2010)
33. Shannon, P., et al.: Cytoscape: a software environment for integrated models of biomolecular interaction networks. Genome Res. **13**(11), 2498–2504 (2003)
34. Sievert, C., et al.: plotly: Create interactive web graphics via "plotly. js". r package version 4.7. 1 (2017)
35. Song, X., Zhou, S., Zhang, Y., Liu, Y., Zhu, H., Gao, J.H.: Frequency-dependent modulation of regional synchrony in the human brain by eyes open and eyes closed resting-states. PloS ONE **10**(11), e0141507 (2015)
36. Sporns, O.: Network attributes for segregation and integration in the human brain. Curr. Opin. Neurobiol. **23**(2), 162–171 (2013)
37. Stanley, M.L., Moussa, M.N., Paolini, B., Lyday, R.G., Burdette, J.H., Laurienti, P.J.: Defining nodes in complex brain networks. Front. Comput. Neurosci. **7**, 169 (2013)
38. Tzourio-Mazoyer, N., et al.: Automated anatomical labeling of activations in SPM using a macroscopic anatomical parcellation of the MNI MRI single-subject brain. Neuroimage **15**(1), 273–289 (2002)
39. Van Den Heuvel, M.P., Pol, H.E.H.: Exploring the brain network: a review on resting-state fMRI functional connectivity. Eur. Neuropsychopharmacol. **20**(8), 519–534 (2010)
40. Wang, J., Wang, X., Xia, M., Liao, X., Evans, A., He, Y.: GRETNA: a graph theoretical network analysis toolbox for imaging connectomics. Front. Hum. Neurosci. **9**, 386 (2015)
41. Xia, M., Wang, J., He, Y.: BrainNet viewer: a network visualization tool for human brain connectomics. PloS ONE **8**(7), e68910 (2013)
42. Zuo, X.N., et al.: Growing together and growing apart: regional and sex differences in the lifespan developmental trajectories of functional homotopy. J. Neurosci. **30**(45), 15034–15043 (2010)

A Network Embedding Approach for Link Prediction in Dynamic Networks

Aswathy Divakaran$^{(\boxtimes)}$ and Anuraj Mohan

Department of Computer Science and Engineering, NSS College of Engineering, Palakkad, India
aswathydiv36@gmail.com, anurajmohan@gmail.com

Abstract. Dynamic networks and their evolving nature have gained the attention of researchers with its ubiquitous applications in a variety of real-world scenarios. Learning the evolutionary behavior of such networks is directly related to link prediction problem as the addition and removal of links or edges over time leads to the network evolution. With the rise of large-scale dynamic networks like social networks, link prediction in such networks or otherwise temporal link prediction has become an interesting field of study. Existing techniques for enhancing the performance of temporal link prediction leverages the notion of matrix factorization, likelihood estimation, deep learning and time series based techniques. However, building a framework for temporal link prediction that preserves the non-linear varying temporal properties of dynamic networks is still an open challenge. Here, we propose a unified framework that incorporates Network Representation Learning (NRL) and time series analysis for temporal link prediction. Our experimental results on various real-word datasets show that the proposed framework outperforms the state-of-the-art works.

Keywords: Dynamic networks · Temporal networks · Link prediction · Network Representation Learning (NRL) · Time series

1 Introduction

In the past few years, there have been intensive researches dealing with the study of highly dynamic networks or temporal networks [1] whose topologies or characteristics change as a function of time. Almost all the real-world complex phenomena can be modeled as dynamic networks since they can model the evolving nature quite efficiently. For instance, social networks, communication networks, biological networks etc. have an underlying structure of dynamic networks where entities and relationships are relatively short and instantaneous. Recently, the evolutionary behavior of such networks gained the attention of researchers with its ubiquitous applications in a variety of real-world scenarios. Moreover, learning the evolutionary behavior is directly related to the link prediction problem [5] as the addition and removal of edges or links over time leads to the network evolution. With the rise of large-scale dynamic networks, link prediction in such networks also known as temporal link prediction has become an interesting field of study. The goal of this task is to predict the links in the network that would appear in its

© Springer Nature Singapore Pte Ltd. 2020
S. Balusamy et al. (Eds.): ICC3 2019, CCIS 1213, pp. 18–28, 2020.
https://doi.org/10.1007/978-981-15-9700-8_2

future state of time under the assumption that the network is complete. Unlike missing link prediction in static networks, temporal link prediction is a challenging task driven by its ubiquitous applications in a variety of scenarios. Recommending new products in e-bay or amazon, friend suggestions in online social networks are some of the obvious examples. In biological networks, predicting the interactions between molecules at a specific time stamp can help us better understand the temporal interaction between them. This can provide useful temporal information that indicate the stage of a specific disease such as cancer. Therefore temporal link prediction plays an important role in disease prediction task. In addition, this task can be used to predict the academic collaborations in co-authorship and citation networks. Furthermore, temporal link prediction in terrorist communication networks help us to predict and capture the most important information related to the issue of national security.

The advancements in deep learning has shown its outstanding performance in various fields like financial services, health care, etc. to find better and faster decisions in today's data-driven world. The rapid growth of deep learning techniques extended its utility towards the area of social network analysis. Using the deep layers of non-linear transformation, deep learning integrated this field to better capture the non-linear varying temporal patterns in dynamic networks. Recent trends in exploring such patterns leverages the notion of Network Representation Learning (NRL) techniques [2–4] that embeds nodes in the network into a low-dimensional vector space by preserving structural proximities of the network. The key idea behind this technique is to generate continuous vector space representations for nodes in the network in such a way that the structural proximity is preserved. Such representations of real-world networks encode social relations in a continuous vector space and enables the original network to be exploited easily for further analysis. This lead to the emergence of various network embedding approaches for temporal link prediction rather than the computationally intensive Matrix Factorization (MF), Maximum Likelihood (ML) approaches. Furthermore, time series analysis is a well-studied area that aims at revealing significant statistics and characteristics of data. The key idea is to extract the underlying structure of the observed data. Time series can best capture the change over time under the assumption that past events are good starting points for the prediction of future. Time series forecasting aims at predicting the future scores based on the previously observed time series scores. Moreover, the frequently evolving nature of dynamic networks makes time series a promising option for temporal link prediction. Several works deployed time series forecasting for temporal link prediction [6–8].

In general, the movements to enhance the performance of temporal link prediction depends on the effectiveness in capturing the evolving nature of dynamic networks and extracting the non-linear varying temporal patterns. However, building a unified model that preserves all the complex non-linear varying patterns in dynamic networks is an open challenge. To address this challenge, we propose a unified framework that incorporates NRL techniques and time series analysis for link prediction in dynamic networks. Initially, we take snapshots of the network at regular intervals of time to capture the evolving nature. Inspired by NRL techniques, we extract the complex features in dynamic networks by preserving the network properties. This information is incorporated into time series analysis where the time series for each node pair is constructed and future scores are predicted. Link prediction task is performed based on the predicted scores.

2 Problem Definition

This section provides a formal definition for temporal link prediction. "Let $G = (V, E)$ be a dynamic network, where V is the set of vertices and each edge $(u, v) \in E$ represents a link between u and v. Given the snapshots of G represented as $G_1, G_2, ..., G_t$ from time step 1 to t, how can we predict the network for a next time step G_{t+1}?" Fig. 1 depicts an overview of temporal link prediction.

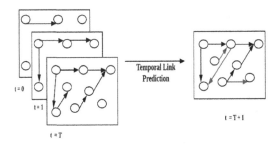

Fig. 1. Overview of temporal link prediction

3 Related Works

The literature in the field of temporal link prediction can be broadly classified into six based on the techniques used: Matrix Factorization (MF) models, probabilistic models, Deep Learning (DL) models, time series based models and others. MF or otherwise called matrix factorization techniques aims at decomposing a matrix into its factors and thereby makes complex operations easier. Majority of the works on matrix factorization based temporal link prediction deploy Non-negative Matrix Factorization (NMF) technique [13–16]. Probabilistic models deploy maximum likelihood approaches or probability distributions instead of fixed values. There exists several probabilistic models for temporal link prediction [17, 18]. A few works on temporal link prediction rests on spectral graph theory, which is the study of properties of a graph in relationship to the eigenvalues and eigenvectors associated with the graph [9, 10].

Time series based temporal link prediction deploys various time series forecasting models for predicting links in the network for a future time period. Time series score is constructed by computing various similarity measures between each node pairs in the network. Time series forecasting aims at predicting the future scores based on the previously observed time series scores. Time series based temporal link prediction frameworks take the adjacency and occurrence matrices corresponding to each snapshot network as input and performs temporal link prediction in three steps: node similarity score computation, node similarity score prediction and link prediction. Univariate time series based temporal link prediction [6] takes into account node's local neighborhood based similarity measures. Unlike univariate time series models, multivariate time series link prediction models [7, 8] integrate temporal evolution of the network, node similarities and node connectivity information. Deep learning (DL) also called deep structured learning has shown its outstanding performance in various real-world scenarios. Using the deep layers of non-linear transformation, deep learning integrated this field to better capture the non-linear varying temporal patterns in dynamic networks. Recent advancements in DL leverages the notion of NRL for temporal link prediction. NRL or otherwise graph embedding techniques eliminated the need for painstaking feature engineering. The goal of this approach is to represent a graph in a low-dimensional vector space by preserving all the network properties. Different algorithms for graph embedding differs in the way they preserve all the network properties. A very few works in temporal link prediction concentrated on modelling an RBM [11].

This study revealed that there exists several NRL techniques which gives the latent representations for nodes in the network by preserving the local and global properties. In addition, the frequently changing nature of dynamic networks make time series a promising option for temporal link prediction. There exists several techniques based on time series analysis for temporal link prediction. However, all of them deploy neighborhood based similarity measures and thereby ignores the global properties of the network. Here, we propose a unified framework that incorporates NRL techniques and time series analysis for temporal link prediction.

4 Proposed Method

In this section, we introduce the proposed network embedding approach for time series based temporal link prediction. Our framework incorporates NRL based techniques and time series for temporal link prediction. The general architecture of proposed framework given in Fig. 2 is composed of four major phases: Network Representation Learning, Time Series Construction, Time Series Forecasting, Link Prediction. Initially, snapshots of the evolving network is taken at regular intervals of time. This enables to analyze the network structure for consecutive time periods.

4.1 Network Representation Learning (NRL)

NRL has been inspired from the language modeling techniques where words are replaced by nodes in the network. This methodology maps network vertices into a low-dimensional vector space, where all the network properties are preserved. Given a network $G = (V, E)$, NRL finds a mapping function $\Phi: v \in V \rightarrow \mathbb{R}^{|V| \times D}$, where $D << |V|$, such that every node $v \in V$ is mapped into a D-dimensional vector space by preserving the structural proximity among nodes. Such latent representations of real-world networks encode social relations in a continuous vector space. This facilitates the original network to be easily deployed for further analysis. In the proposed framework, we deploy the most recent NRL techniques such as Node2Vec [3], SDNE [2] and DNGR [4]. Figure 3 depicts the latent representation of a network obtained using SDNE method.

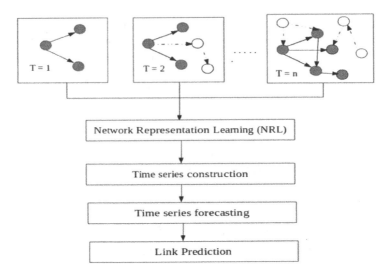

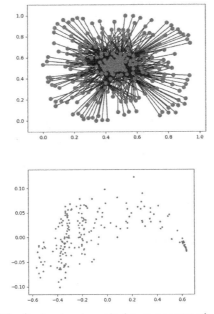

Fig. 2. Architecture diagram

Fig. 3. A network and its latent representation

Node2Vec is an algorithmic framework that leverages the notion of random walks that preserves the network neighborhood of nodes to learn continuous feature representations for nodes in the network. The feature learning framework is introduced by extending the SkipGram architecture which optimizes the objective function given by

Eq. 1, where $N_S(u)$ is the neighborhood of node u and f is the feature representation of the corresponding node.

$$\max_f \sum_{u \in V} \log Pr(N_S(u)|f(u)) \tag{1}$$

SDNE is a semi-supervised framework that captures the highly non-linear structure of the networks. Inspired from the recent advancements in DL, this framework utilized deep autoencoders for learning latent representation of the network. Autoencoders have a deep neural network architecture and is composed of two parts: encoder and decoder. The encoder module is composed of multiple non-linear functions that maps the input data into its corresponding representation space. Decoder also consists of multiple non-linear functions that map the representations into a reconstruction space. SDNE exploits the first and second order proximities of the network to distinguish between the global and local network structure. This enables to learn the latent representations by preserving the structural proximities of the network.

DNGR is also an autoencoder based NRL framework. The model consists of a random surfing and context weighting module that generates the probabilistic distribution of the co-occurrence matrix and Stacked Denoising Autoencoder (SDAE) for dimensionality reduction. Given a network, DNGR performs a random surfing process (similar to PageRank) to generate a weighted co-occurrence matrix followed by the construction of Positive Pointwise Mutual Information (PPMI). This matrix contains the structural information of the network and it is given to SDAE to generate the latent representation for the network by optimizing the following objective function (see Eq. 2), where x_i is the input data and $h(y_i; \theta)$ is the reconstructed data.

$$argmin_\theta \sum_{i=1}^{n} ||x_i - h(y_i; \theta)|| \tag{2}$$

4.2 Time Series Construction and Forecasting

Time series construction phase takes as input the node embeddings obtained in the previous phase. For each pair of nodes, a similarity score is computed based on their low-dimensional node vectors. Let $\Phi_t(u)$ and $\Phi_t(v)$ be the embeddings of two nodes u and v respectively at time t, cosine similarity is defined as:

$$Cos_{sim} = \frac{\Phi_t(u).\Phi_t(v)}{|\Phi_t(u)||\Phi_t(v)|} \tag{3}$$

In addition to the similarity score computation, we analyze the change over time by modeling a time series for each pair of nodes. The cosine similarity scores of node pairs over time represented as time series enables to characterize the change in position of nodes in the embedding space.

The time series thus constructed is taken as input for time series forecasting phase. In the proposed system, we deploy ARIMA model [12] which maximizes the likelihood function. Once the time series is constructed, the future score values are predicted using

ARIMA (p, d, q) model. For a pair of nodes (u, v), the model which is applied to predict the score for time t by considering p autoregressive terms and q moving average terms is given by Eq. 4, where Φ_i and θ_j represents constant terms and ϵ_t is the white noise. ARIMA model is applied with different p, d, q values. The parameter values giving minimum Akaike Information Criteria (AIC) value are utilized for predicting the future score values for each node pair.

$$\text{Score}(u, v, t) = \sum_{i=1}^{p} \Phi_i \text{Score}(u, v, t - i) + \sum_{j=1}^{q} \theta_j \epsilon_{t-j} + \epsilon_t \qquad (4)$$

4.3 Link Prediction

In this phase, the future time series scores estimated in the previous phase are used to predict how likely two given nodes are to connect in future. First, each node pair are sorted based on the predicted similarity score. The sorted list is compared with actual links in the network for a future time.

5 Experiments

In this section we conduct experiments on several real-world datasets to evaluate the performance of the proposed temporal link prediction framework. Here, we utilize suitable evaluation measures to compare the accuracy of the method with the baseline methods under different scenarios. All the experiments were conducted on a machine with 15.6 GiB RAM and hexa-core processor with 3.2 GHz speed.

5.1 Datasets Used

Various standard real-world datasets are available to evaluate the performance of temporal link prediction. The following datasets were used in our experiments.

1. **Enron:** This dataset consists of emails between the employees in Enron Inc. from January 1999 to July 2002. Each node in the network represents a user and a link represents email communication between them.
2. **Haggle:** This network describes human contact information where contacts between people are measured by some wireless devices. Nodes represents users and links between them indicates a contact.
3. **Hep-ph:** This a collaboration graph of authors of scientific papers from Hep-Ph section of arXiv archive. The data covers papers in the period from January 1993 to April 2003.
4. **Radoslaw:** This network represents the email communication between employees in a mid-sized manufacturing company. Nodes in the network represents employees and edges between them are individual emails.

Table 1 shows the statistics of the datasets used. For Hep-ph dataset, we consider only the most popular nodes and it consists of 265 nodes and 19,736 edges. All the other datasets are used as it is.

Table 1. Statistics of the datasets used

Dataset	#Nodes	#Edges	#Timestamps
Enron	150	150	27
Haggle	274	274	6
Hep-ph	28,093	28,093	9
Radoslaw	167	167	10

5.2 Results and Analysis

The proposed framework is compared with some of the state-of-the-art works to evaluate the performance. The evaluation metrics used are Area Under the Curve (AUC) [16, 19] and Mean Average Precision (MAP) [2]. First, the system is compared with static link prediction techniques. Second, the evaluation of the proposed framework with state-of-the-art time series based temporal link prediction techniques is performed. Moreover, the effect of various network embedding techniques on the proposed framework is also observed. In this paper, static techniques are denoted as st-cn, st-jc, st-aa and the proposed time series based framework is denoted as ts-node2vec, ts-sdne and ts-dngr.

Comparison with Static Link Prediction Techniques
On comparing the time series based framework which deploy local similarity indices and proposed framework on static link prediction techniques, it was found that the time series based approaches gives a better prediction results. Figure 4(a) shows that time series based local similarity metrics (ts-aa) for temporal link prediction improves the AUC scores for static link prediction using local similarity metrics (st-aa) by 14.75%, 29.09%, 18.3% and 32.7% for Enron, Haggle, Hep-ph and Radoslaw datasets respectively. In addition, the proposed framework (ts-node2vec, ts-sdne, ts-dngr) gives better AUC scores than that for static network embedding techniques (st-node2vec, st-sdne, st-dngr). The result shows that the time series based temporal link prediction techniques performs better than static link prediction techniques which depends solely on static network at a particular time period.

Comparison with Time Series of Neighborhood Based Similarity Metrics
The MAP scores obtained on comparing the proposed framework with state-of-the-art time series based techniques is shown in Table 2. Better prediction results are obtained by taking top 20% links as connected and the rest as disconnected links. The observed results on evaluating the performance of proposed framework in terms of the AUC value computed is depicted in Fig. 4(b). The proposed system shows better results than time series based method using neighborhood based similarity measures for all the four real-world datasets. This confirms that the ability of NRL techniques to generate deep and latent representations of the network improves the prediction results.

Effect of Various Network Embedding Approaches
The performance of the system on three recent network embedding techniques are compared here. The observation of the prediction results on various embedding techniques

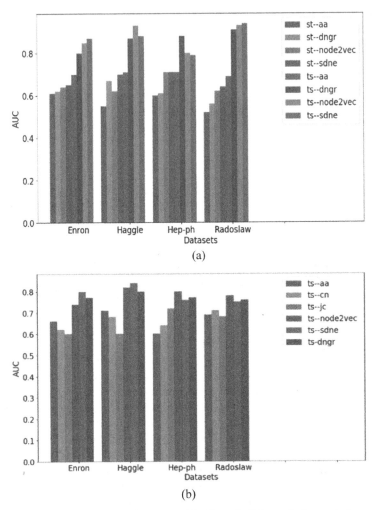

Fig. 4. Comparison of the proposed system with (a) static link prediction techniques (b) time series based link prediction techniques

is shown in Fig. 5. Among the three network embedding techniques, SDNE gives better prediction results for Enron and Haggle datasets. The feature dimension for SDNE is set as d = 16 for both the datasets. Since SDNE is found to be suitable for capturing non-linear patterns, it confirms that joint objective function of autoencoder designed for SDNE better captures the local and global structures in Enron and Haggle networks quite efficiently. Moreover, Node2Vec framework gives a better prediction result for Hep-ph and Radoslaw datasets. For this experiment, the feature dimension for Node2Vec is set as d = 128 for both the datasets. It confirms that the random walk based approach in Node2Vec better captures the community structure in these networks effectively and hence gives a better prediction result.

Table 2. Comparison of MAP scores of proposed system with baseline methods

Method	Enron	Haggle	Hep-ph	Radoslaw
Ts-cn	0.04	0.07	0.03	0.04
Ts-jc	0.06	0.10	0.04	0.03
Ts-aa	0.04	0.06	0.02	0.04
Ts-node2vec	**0.09**	**0.11**	**0.07**	**0.09**
Ts-sdne	**0.08**	**0.30**	**0.05**	**0.08**
Ts-dngr	**0.12**	**0.19**	**0.06**	**0.17**

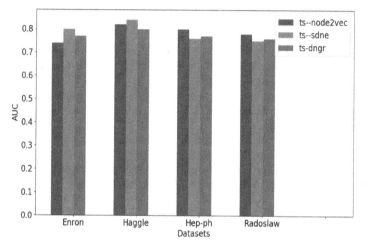

Fig. 5. Effect of various network embedding approaches

6 Conclusion

In this paper, we proposed a unified framework for temporal link prediction which incorporated NRL based techniques and time series analysis. One of the key idea of our framework is to capture the non-linear temporal patterns in dynamic networks using network embedding techniques. Moreover, the framework is extended to incorporate time series forecasting models for prediction, since time series best captures the change over time. Experiments conducted on four real-world datasets show that the proposed system outperforms the state-of-the-art works. In future, the static network embedding techniques can be extended to incorporate dynamic behavior of networks. Dynamic network embeddings techniques can be deployed to perform the temporal link prediction task. The strength of dynamic network embedding techniques can be incorporated for time series construction to yield better prediction results. Moreover, leveraging different neural network models like LSTM for time series forecasting is also an interesting direction towards enhancing the performance of time series based temporal link prediction.

References

1. Holme, P., Saramäki, J.: Temporal networks. Phys. Rep. **519**(3), 97–125 (2012)
2. Wang, D., Cui, P., Zhu, W.: Structural deep network embedding. In: Proceedings of the 22nd ACM SIGKDD International Conference on Knowledge Discovery and Data Mining, pp. 1225–1234 (2016)
3. Grover, A., Leskovec, J.: node2vec: scalable feature learning for networks. In: Proceedings of the 22nd ACM SIGKDD International Conference on Knowledge Discovery and Data Mining, pp. 855–864 (2016)
4. Cao, S., Lu, W., Xu, Q.: Deep neural networks for learning graph representations. In: Thirtieth AAAI Conference on Artificial Intelligence (2016)
5. Liben-Nowell, D., Kleinberg, J.: The link-prediction problem for social networks. J. Am. Soc. Inf. Sci. Technol. **58**(7), 1019–1031 (2007)
6. Güneş, İ., Gündüz-Öğüdücü, Ş., Çataltepe, Z.: Link prediction using time series of neighborhood-based node similarity scores. Data Min. Knowl. Discov. **30**(1), 147–180 (2015). https://doi.org/10.1007/s10618-015-0407-0
7. Özcan, A., Öğüdücü, Ş.G.: Temporal link prediction using time series of quasi-local node similarity measures. In: 2016 15th IEEE International Conference on Machine Learning and Applications (ICMLA), pp. 381–386 (2016)
8. Özcan, A., Öğüdücü, Ş.G.: Multivariate temporal link prediction in evolving social networks. In: 2015 IEEE/ACIS 14th International Conference on Computer and Information Science (ICIS), pp. 185–190 (2015)
9. Wu, T., Chang, C.S., Liao, W.: Tracking network evolution and their applications in structural network analysis. IEEE Trans. Netw. Sci. Eng. (2018)
10. Ralescu, A., Kohram, M.: Spectral regression with low-rank approximation for dynamic graph link prediction. IEEE Intell. Syst. **26**(4), 48–53 (2011)
11. Li, T., Wang, B., Jiang, Y., Zhang, Y., Yan, Y.: Restricted Boltzmann machine-based approaches for link prediction in dynamic networks. IEEE Access **6**, 29940–29951 (2018)
12. Brockwell, P.J., Davis, R.A., Calder, M.V.: Introduction to Time Series and Forecasting, vol. 2. Springer, New York (2002)
13. Lei, K., Qin, M., Bai, B., Zhang, G.: Adaptive multiple non-negative matrix factorization for temporal link prediction in dynamic networks. In: Proceedings of the 2018 Workshop on Network Meets AI & ML, pp. 28–34 (2018)
14. Ma, X., Sun, P., Qin, G.: Nonnegative matrix factorization algorithms for link prediction temporal networks using graph communicability. Pattern Recognit. **71**, 361–374 (2017)
15. Ma, X., Sun, P., Wang, Y.: Graph regularized nonnegative matrix factorization for temporal link prediction in dynamic networks. Phys. Stat. Mech. Appl. **496**, 121–136 (2018)
16. Dunlavy, D.M., Kolda, T.G., Acar, E.: Temporal link prediction using matrix and tensor factorizations. ACM Trans. Knowl. Discov. Data (TKDD) **5**(2), 10 (2011)
17. Das, S., Das, S.K.: A probabilistic link prediction model in time-varying social networks. In 2017 IEEE International Conference on Communications (ICC), pp. 1–6 (2017)
18. Ahamed, N.M., Chen, L.: An efficient algorithm for link prediction in temporal uncertain social networks. Inf. Sci. **331**, 120–136 (2016)
19. Lü, L., Jin, C.H., Zhou, T.: Similarity index based on local paths for link prediction of complex networks. Phys. Rev. E **80**(4), 046122 (2009)

IDK My Friends: Link Analysis on Social Networks to Mine Surprise Connections

Sai Praveen Mylavarapu and Shubhashri Govindarajan[✉]

PSG College of Technology, Coimbatore 641004, India
saipraveenmylavarapu@gmail.com, agshubhashri@gmail.com

Abstract. Social media plays a vital role in connecting people all around the world through various walks and phases of life, forming clustered meaningful communities. However, there is more scope for the social media platforms to mine fine-grained information that can entice and surprise the social media users based upon their respective egocentric networks. The list of mutual friends in an individual's social network might be trivial or obvious most of the time. To up the game and surprise the individuals, the social media platforms could mine those mutual connections that are connected across different communities, serving as inter-cluster crucial edges between communities. As these connections are across the communities, the user possibly wouldn't be aware of these connections and thus would be surprised to know them.

This work contributes along the lines of deploying community detection algorithms like Girvan Newman and graph based modelling techniques to produce the optimal number of surprise connections. This model was tested on real world Twitter based egocentric networks of 156 college students with evidence and survey, showcasing a good performance in surprising users,thereby increasing the interaction and engaging time of users on the social media platform significantly.

Keywords: Link analysis · Graph modelling · Egocentric network · Community detection · Social network · Twitter · Data mining · Computational modelling · Modularity · Divisive hierarchical clustering

1 Introduction

Social network analysis has witnessed a huge wave of attention and improvement in recent years. It has become highly competitive for the social media platform to engage and keep their users excited and involved for more amount of time. To aid and up the game of these platforms, mining and deriving more knowledge from the egocentric networks of the individuals is one of the ways to move forward.

This work revolves around the idea of surprising social media users by notifying them of the connections that are unknown to them in their friends' circle. In this paper, we define surprise connections of a person to be two of the person's friends who belong to different communities in the person's egocentric network and are friends with each other. A community characterizes a set of nodes that are densely connected amongst themselves and sparsely connected with other nodes in the network.

S. P. Mylavarapu and S. Govindarajan—Both the authors contributed equally to this work.

© Springer Nature Singapore Pte Ltd. 2020
S. Balusamy et al. (Eds.): ICC3 2019, CCIS 1213, pp. 29–35, 2020.
https://doi.org/10.1007/978-981-15-9700-8_3

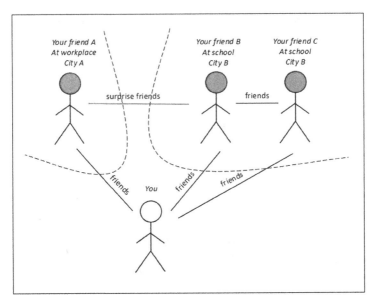

Fig. 1. Surprise connections in IDK My Friends

Figure 1 portrays the significance of this research work. Say, B and C were your school friends. As you moved on to work in another city, A became your good friend at the workplace. Say, A and B had met at a tech conference and were friends ever since. Our research work helps you to discover the potential surprise connection that A and B are friends with each other which you are unaware of. Indeed this a surprise connection when compared to a trivially known connection that B and C are friends too. Mining these types of connections from the individual's egocentric network is the aim of IDK my friends.

As an example, if a person has 400 friends with 4 communities in his/her network, the number of connections may be around 19,000 assuming the clusters are highly connected. Out of all these connections, we aim to mine only those connections that the user may not be aware of, which could be probably 3 or 4 connections.

To the best of our knowledge, no one has studied techniques to mine connections that surprise users. We have modeled this problem as a graph and applied community detection algorithms and its variants to detect the optimum number of inter cluster edges between dense communities, thus notifying them as the surprise connections. This work also contributes in obtaining the ideal number of connections that are the only connections that surprise the user.

2   IDK My Friends

2.1   Dataset Preprocessing

A 1.5 degree egocentric network [1] of a person is a network from that person's point of view in which all the people with whom this person is connected are taken and all ties among these people are included. Using the Python library Tweepy [2], Twitter's API [3] responses are obtained and a 1.5 degree egocentric network of the user is constructed. Initially, the information of people that the user is 'following' is retrieved. For every person in the list of 'following' people, the ids of the people he/she is 'following' is immediately fetched and returned. These ids are the friends of friends of the user. The same is done for the followers who follow back the "following" people of the user. An intersection of these two sets of ids, forms the friendship ties and connections in the network. On an average, a total of around 925 nodes and 22500 edges were present in the egocentric graphs of an individual. The node represents the friend of the user and edges represent connections between friends.

Since the graph represents the connections and ties between the alters, it is an undirected and unweighted graph. Given the fact that the data is from a social media platform, the network's nodes cluster around various communities like school, family, work and from other walks and phases of life.

2.2 Approach

Girvan Newman algorithm [4], a divisive hierarchical clustering based algorithm, with numerous variations and optimizations was used to detect the ideal number of clustered communities without the user specified, desirable number of clusters. The complex network of friends circle was represented as a graph with the people as nodes and edges connecting friends. Girvan Newman algorithm uses the edge betweenness factor to iteratively eliminate edges through which the highest number of shortest paths between nodes in the graph pass through. These edges have high edge betweenness factor that serve as potential surprise connections.

The optimal number of inter cluster edges that have to be considered (surprise connections) forms the main crux of the problem statement. Instead of using a hyper-parameter for number of clusters, we employed the concept of modularity to aid in producing potential surprise connections until more fine-grained, communities emerge, still maintaining a high cohesion within clusters [5].

$$\text{Modularity, Q} = \text{(number of edges within groups)} -$$
$$\text{(Expected number of edges within groups)}$$

Actual number of edges between node i and node j is,

$$\text{Aij} = 1, \text{ if there is an edge between node i and node j}$$
$$= 0, \text{ otherwise}$$

Expected number of edges between node i and node j is, $\frac{k_i k_j}{2m}$, where k_i is degree of node i and k_j is degree of node j and m is the number of edges in the cluster.
Thus,

$$Q = \frac{1}{4m} \left[\sum_{i,j} \left(A_{ij} - \frac{k_i k_j}{2m} \right) \delta(c_i, c_j) \right] \tag{1}$$

where c_i is group id of Node i and c_j is group id of Node j and

$$\delta(a,b) = 1, \text{if} \quad a=b$$
$$= 0 \text{ otherwise.}$$

Q lies in the range [-1, 1] and is calculated for all groups and aggregated. If Q > 0,number of edges within the group exceeds the expected number of edges within the group. The surprise connections are produced until the optimal Q is reached. In practice, for networks with strong community structure, Q typically falls in the range of 0.3 to 0.7 [6].

The algorithm's steps to retrieve surprise connections are listed below:

1. Compute the edge betweeness of all existing edges in the network.
2. Remove the edge with the highest edge betweenness serving as a surprise connection across communities.
3. Recompute the edge betweeness of edges affected after the removal of this edge.
4. Steps 2 and 3 are repeated until optimal Q is reached.

Unlike the clustering or partitioning algorithms that require a hyper-parameter "k", to stop partitioning after user-defined number of communities are obtained, this algorithm stops when the optimum fine-grained communities are formed. The computing time efficiency is better off when compared to the naive methods as the edge betweeness of the affected edges are the only edges for which recomputation occurs and this whole procedure stops when the optimum "k" is reached without validating on a range of values to find the optimum number of clusters. In order to improve scalability and compute time, the fast optimized version of the Girvan Newman algorithm was employed into the application, as discussed in the next section.

2.3 Variations and Optimizations

The fast optimized version of Girvan Newman algorithm [7] was used to increase the scalability and computing time efficiency by considering the matrix format of Q as,

$$Q = \frac{1}{4m} \sum_{i,j} \left(A_{ij} - \frac{k_i k_j}{2m} \right) s_i s_j = \frac{1}{4m} \left(s^T B s \right) \tag{2}$$

where, Nodes i and j are considered from the same group
   s is a vector of group memberships such that $s_i \in \{+1, -1\}$
   B is the modularity matrix,

$$B_{ij} = A_{ij} - \frac{k_i k_j}{2m} \tag{3}$$

Q is maximized to find s, by rewriting Q in terms of eigenvalues of B and dividing the nodes of the elements of the leading eigenvector of B hierarchically until the proposed split does not increase modularity [8].

Steps for the fast optimized version to retrieve surprise connections are listed below:

1. Finding the leading eigenvector of modularity matrix, B
2. Divide the nodes by the sign of the elements in the leading eigenvector
3. Repeat hierarchically until:

   A. If a current proposed split does not cause modularity to increase, declare community not divisible and revert back to previous state
   B. If not A, the inter cluster edges obtained are potential surprise connections.

4. If all communities are indivisible, end.

The eigenvector is computed by using the power method, by initially starting with a random value until it converges through iterative multiplication and normalization.

3 Experimental Results

A web application using the fast optimized version of Girvan Newman algorithm was developed using Python, NetworkX library [9] and Twitter APIs to obtain the egocentric network of the user.

A total of 156 students from a college have used the web application and have taken up a survey to verify if the surprise connections generated by our application indeed surprised them or not (the user already knows that they are friends), or the user did not know much about those connections (befriended casually). The average size of the individual network contains 925 nodes and 22500 edges. On an average, every person was given 5 - 6 surprise connections.

Table 1 summarizes the corresponding survey results. Global response row is the percentage calculated from the total sum of responses by all users. The percentage of surprise connections is calculated for every user and these individual percentages are added up to generate an average across all users. Average individual response row contains these results. This is to evaluate if some users found most results surprising while others hardly found the connections as surprising. The results didn't deviate much showing that this is not the case.

Table 1. Experimental results of the web application, IDK my friends.

Metric	# responses	Surprised	Not surprised	Did not know
Global response	860	96.28%	1.63%	2.09%
Avg individual response	5.5	96.58%	2.14%	1.28%

As the results show that 96.28% of the responses are surprising, we infer that the algorithm stops when the optimal number of clusters are identified.

The sub-figures in Fig. 2 show an example of the visual representation of a user's egocentric network from Twitter. There are four distinct communities detected, namely high school, junior college, college and family which go hand-in-hand with real time

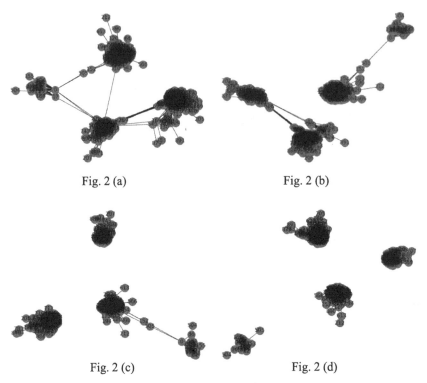

Fig. 2 (a)   Fig. 2 (b)

Fig. 2 (c)   Fig. 2 (d)

Fig. 2. Graph visualization of community detection for a sample user.

data of the user who was an undergraduate student. The surprise connections are the inter cluster edges that are being removed at each stage.

4   Other Applications

The proposed method in this work has great potential to be applied in different domains. One such application would be to find out people who work on particular cross-domain fields on GitHub or other repository hosting service projects (a repository can belong to multiple domains, for example, medicine, banking, machine learning, etc.). Other applications may include, anomaly detection in networks,detecting sudden switch between tasks or user behavior in a network, studying patterns in biochemical networks and observing movement of people across different groups of companies to understand the human thought process and psychology in life.

5   Conclusion and Future Work

We conclude that the fast optimization algorithm to find crucial inter cluster edges as surprise connections performs well to a large extent on large egocentric networks of common users on social media platforms. The algorithm deployed provides an apt threshold to stop generating surprise connections when an ideal modularity factor is reached. This serves as an advantage over clustering and partitioning algorithms that rely upon a user defined number of clusters. The fast optimization algorithm has caused a good amount of speed up in the compute time and has improved the scalability substantially.

The future works include increasing the scalability as millions of users would concurrently want to access their egocentric networks to figure out the surprise connections. Possible approaches to tackle this problem would be to execute the deployed code on the client's browser rather than on server side, use distributed computing techniques or consider finding an optimum threshold for the surprise connections with factors, namely local random walk [10] along with modularity or tackling the problem without a community detection approach.

References

1. Hogan, B.: Visualizing and interpreting facebook networks. In: Analyzing Social Media Networks with NodeXL, Insights from a Connected World. Amsterdam, Elsevier, pp. 165–179 (2011) https://doi.org/10.1016/B978-0-12-382229-1.00011-4
2. "API Reference." API Reference-Tweepy 3.5.0 Documentation. Retrieved from https://docs.tweepy.org/en/v3.5.0/api.html
3. "Docs-Twitter Developers". Retrieved from https://developer.twitter.com/en/docs.html
4. Girvan, M., Newman, M.E.J.: Community structure in social and biological networks. Proc. Natl. Acad. Sci. 99(12), 7821–7826 (2002)
5. Qi, X., Song, H., Wu, J., Fuller, E., Luo, R., Zhang, C.Q.: Eb&D: a new clustering approach for signed social networks based on both edge-betweenness centrality and density of subgraphs. Elsevier Phys. A. Stat. Mech. Appl. 482, 147–157 (2017)
6. Newman, M.E.J., Girvan, M.: Finding and evaluating community structure in networks. Physical Review E, USA, American Physical Society. 69 26–113 (2004)
7. Newman, M.E.J.: Fast algorithm for detecting community structure in networks. In: Physical Review E, USA, American Physical Society. 69, 66–133(2004)
8. Newman, M.E.J.: Finding community structure in networks using the eigenvectors of matrices. Physical Review E, USA, American Physical Society. 74(3), 36–104 (2006)
9. Hagberg, A., Swart, P., S Chult, D.: Exploring network structure, dynamics, and function using NetworkX. In Gäel Varoquaux, Travis Vaught, and Jarrod Millman (Eds), Proceedings of the 7th Python in Science Conference (SciPy2008). Pasadena, CA USA, pp 11–15 (2008)
10. Liu, D., Wang, C., Jing, Y.: Estimating the optimal number of communities by cluster analysis. Int. J. Modern Phys. B, 30, p. 1650037 (2016)

Prediction of Patient Readmission Using Machine Learning Techniques

V. Diviya Prabha and R. Rathipriya$^{(\boxtimes)}$

Department of Computer Science, Periyar University, Salem 11, India
diviyaprabha7@gmail.com, rathipriyar@gmail.com

Abstract. Prediction analysis on hospital readmission has become perplexing due to large volume of data. In today's world, data generated from hospitals, sensors, reports from doctor, etc., accurate readmission prediction for large dataset is a challenging task. The aim of this paper is to develop an accurate prediction model for readmission to improve healthcare. A new approach called Entropy Based Feature Selection and Entropy Based Hyper Parameter Tuning for Logistic Regression is developed for accurate prediction of readmission and enhances machine performance for large dataset. The evaluation shows the proposed model provides accuracy of 96% comparatively greater than other models and less computation time.

Keywords: Decision making · Predictive analytics · Machine learning · Logistic regression

1 Introduction

Data mining is the process of finding relevant patterns from large size of historical data. The data mining approach is classified from Artificial Intelligence and machine learning (Islam et al. 2018) techniques. The main aim of data mining is prediction it is the most common application used in many areas. It is also process of finding relationship between variables in order to identify new patterns. Hospital readmission is turned great attention to patient and doctors. It is defined as return of patient soon after the discharge less than of 30 days. Survey results 2,599 hospitals (Brindise and Steele, Machine Learning-based Pre-discharge Prediction of Hospital Readmission, IEEE 2018) will face the problem of readmission rate. Excessive readmission is increasing day-by-day which leads to negative impact to the healthcare patients. The main causes are chronic disease, heart attack, hip and knee replacement and pneumonia. As patient data is increasing there is no predictive analytics for huge volume of data. Predictive analytics aim to build a model target of learning process. Predictive analytics towards healthcare is a challenging task in today's world. The medicinal field has its incredible commitment in this storm of information on some innovative developments in the field like predictive analytics which has moved the trial of consideration past history of patients self-care and observing utilizing straightforward gadgets that convey results on prediction of disease. It distinguished (Islam et al. 2018) three kinds of investigation in techniques: descriptive

© Springer Nature Singapore Pte Ltd. 2020
S. Balusamy et al. (Eds.): ICC3 2019, CCIS 1213, pp. 36–48, 2020.
https://doi.org/10.1007/978-981-15-9700-8_4

is investigation and disclosure of data in the dataset, predictive is used for forecast of present and future occasions dependent on authentic information and prescriptive use of situations to give choice help.

Management of large volume of data in healthcare is a difficult task it paves a way to Big Data Analytics (Wang and Ann 2016). It consist of more than a terabyte of data (Volume), x-rays, text data (Variety), sensor data like health monitoring for ICU patients (Velocity), patient care (Veracity) etc., that contains different V's performing Big Data. Recently Big Data is misused as volume only that is huge volume of data. It is not only one V of Volume it includes another V's also. The modern Big Data with data mining is used to extract new knowledge from the lots of data at the individual level of patients. The role of analytics is used to improve patient care, diagnosing disease at the early stage, reducing cost and easy way to connect doctor and patient continuously. Huge volume of unstructured data is useful only if it converted into a meaningful way is the task of analytics. Spark is a cluster technology that is the MapReduce concept in Big Data. It works on the concept of RDD (Resilient Distributed Dataset) where the element of dataset works in parallel to reach the solution. Data are useful only if it is proper format and unstable by human. Analytics is doing better in hospitals and urban patient care for data management for upcoming patient. It also provides a way to personalized medicine.

Machine learning is a statistical tool for data analysis for predicting better outcome. It is also a kind of artificial intelligence techniques allows the model to learn automatically. This kind of approach provides a great impact for medical research which has huge amount of data. Diabetes is a high risk disease affecting from just born baby to old age people by high glucose level. Normally the food and drug taken by human is converted to glucose or sugar. A person may have high blood sugar if the production of insulin is insufficient or insulin doesn't respond to body. The International Diabetes Federation (Jayanthi et al. 2017) has reported that by 2045 cases of diabetes will rise to 152 million in India which is regrettable fact. Accurate prediction of readmission is a challenging task in health care problem. As data in healthcare is increasing as hospital and patient get increased maintaining data and prediction of future outcome is a difficult task. To reduce patient readmission and early stage to take care of patient is easy.

The Sect. 2 discusses the review of related work and process of proposed work in readmission prediction. Section 3 describes the machine learning techniques and proposed methodology of readmission prediction model. Section 4 concludes the paper.

2 Methods and Materials

Machine learning techniques for hospital readmission prediction using data driven model is carried out (Lacson et al. 2019) with testing approach was calculated in 5-fold cross validation, features ranking was performed by correlation based feature selection. Patient similarity (Tashkandia et al. 2018) is analyzed with exploration of big data machine learning condition are applied for decision making. 30-day hospital readmission prediction after acute myocardial infarction it identifies early risk of patient the data are collected from 6 hospitals from diverse and proposed method is followed. Numerous methods are tried for readmission prediction but accurate prediction is not an easy task. The machine learning application (Brindise and Steele, Machine Learning-based Pre-discharge Prediction of Hospital Readmission, IEEE 2018) are described and pre-discharge prediction of hospitalreadmission with an accuracy of 71% is obtained. Deep Learning techniques (Hammoudeh et al. 2018) combination of data engineering and convolution neural network are used for prediction which outperforms well. Diabetic patient readmission prediction is an important research in some cases model is not specific to reach the target the focus on ensemble (average) methods to reach the target (Mingle, Predicting Diabetic Readmission Rates: Moving Beyond Hba1c 2017). In this paper (Sneha and Gangil 2019) analyzing diabetic data using machine learning in which navie bayes outperforms the best accuracy of 82%. It takes the correlation value and generates the value of attributes as 1 predicting for both diabetic patient and non-diabetic patient. It also summarizes the importance of optimal features for predictive analytics. The proposed methodology is this paper uses entropy for variable selection and hyperparameter tuning for logistic regression. The existing high-dimensional patient data is reduced with optimal variables. This outperforms better accuracy than the other model. This model also focuses to implement BigData in pyspark aspects. It also suits for increasing data dynamically to handle new data for readmission prediction. It helps to reduce the readmission risk and improves patient care.

3 Machine Learning Techniques

Machine learning is a mathematical model used to extract the insights from data available. It aims to solve critical problems and identify health risk to improve patient care. Machine learning towards healthcare aims to replace doctors and nurse paves a way to personalized prediction. There are different types of machine learning models the model which is high in accuracy for predicting is chosen as best model for prediction. This paper utilizes logistic regression to find the variables (features) that determine readmission prediction accurately.

3.1 Feature Selection

Feature selection also known as variable selection is an important approach for model prediction. To identify the relevant data (Lacson et al. 2019) is an important task to improve the accuracy. The basic feature selection method filter and wrapper methods are already performed (Yifan and Sharma 2014; Cai and Luo 2018). From 36 features 11 features are selected from feature selection method.

Table 1 describes the algorithms such as Principle Component Analysis (PCA), SelectKbest, Extra tree classifier and Entropy are carried out to select the best features for readmission prediction. Among the methods Entropy based Feature Selection (EFS) performs better for readmission prediction.

The Fig. 1 expounds the feature selection using PCA method, the horizontal line indicate the value of each individual feature for readmission the high values features are selected for prediction. Similarly methods SelectKbest and Extra tree classifier are evaluated discrimination of figure was different feature were attempted from each methods.

Table 1. Feature selection using various methods

Algorithms	Features
PCA	(1, 3, 4, 5, 7, 10, 11, 12, 22, 24, 30, 31)
SelectKbest	(1, 5, 7, 10, 11, 12, 14, 22, 31)
Extra Tree Classifier	(1, 3, 6, 8, 12, 14, 30, 31, 35)
EFS	(1, 3, 5, 7, 8, 11, 12, 14, 15, 20, 26)

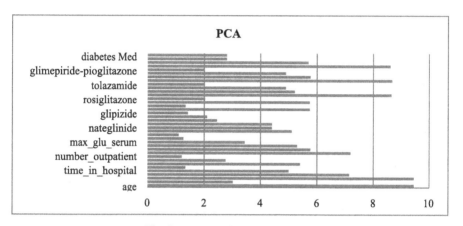

Fig. 1. Feature selection using PCA

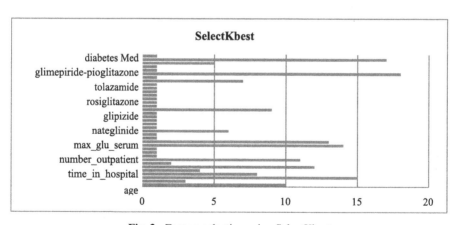

Fig. 2. Feature selection using SelectKbest

In EFS significant whose accuracy is high compared to other methods. It was observed that entropy based feature selection indicate good fit to the prediction model.

The Figs. 2, 3 and 4 epitomizes the feature selection with Principle Component Analysis (PCA), SelectKbest and EFS features are selected based on the readmission

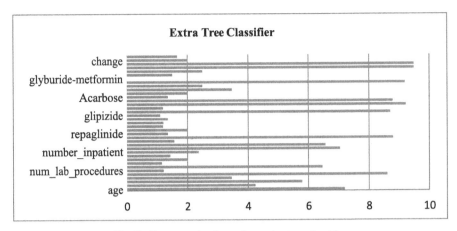

Fig. 3. Feature selection using extra tree classifier

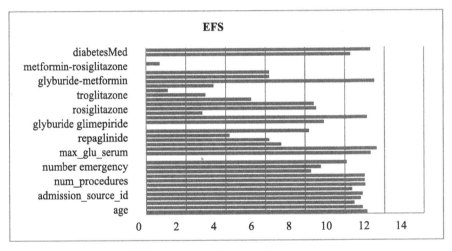

Fig. 4. Feature selection using entropy

prediction. The value of each method differs considerably to enhance the best feature. The value that is greater is taken for the consideration as best features. In the present study EFS provides high accuracy compared to other methods. From this method the 11 features are taken as best feature for readmission prediction. This method proves that a good predictive model needs the best features to improve accuracy. Table 2 defines mean values and Standard Deviation value (S.D). It also mention the estimated S.D and mean value for each features the values are increasing and decreasing based on the features.

3.2 Decision Tree

It is one of the comprehensible classification techniques and one in every of the foremost common learning ways. The illustration of decision tree is dividing the attributes of

Table 2. Mean and S.D values of features

Features	Estimated mean value	S.D	Estimated S.D	S.D mean
age	65.51	0.040	15.97	0.06
time_in_hospital	4.20	0.070	2.93	0.01
num_procedures	1.42	0.004	1.75	0.06
discharge_id	3.47	0.013	5.22	0.09
number_inpatient	0.17	0.001	0.60	0.01
A1Cresult	0.12	0.008	0.33	0.01
metformin	0.21	0.001	0.40	0.01
insulin	0.51	0.001	0.49	0.01
numchange	0.26	0.001	0.48	0.01
num_medications	15.6	0.022	8.28	0.01
glyburide	0.11	0.001	0.31	0.08

dataset into braches until certain condition is satisfied. The first decision tree algorithm was proposed by Ross Quinlan in 1986 (Quinlan 1986).

Decision tree are separated root to inner node called leaf. The stopping common criteria for decision tree are

- The best condition must not overcome a threshold
- The height the tree reached maximum
- The number of nodes is less the minimum value

The instance in Fig. 5 describes if abc is the root of the tree if abc is a1 then it will point to another subset of root def else it might be b1 or c1 to the value of class yes or no similar kind of performance in the root def. The decision tree in healthcare bigdata is an important task such as length of stay in hospital, total cost of hospital etc., (Moon and Lee 2017) the variables are divided into groups and sub-groups to predictive the output with many variables.

3.3 Random Forest

Random Forest algorithm fits several decision tree on dataset and predicts the model accuracy (Lacson et al. 2019). Training the data while building the trees and for splitting nodes are taken into consideration some samples are replaced with multiple times. Randomized tree is used for understanding the variable importance for prediction (Louppe et al. n.d.) pruning the random space is allowed to identify relevant variables. Making the prediction using random forest is to find the correct relevant features is the importance of learning algorithm. Random forest is a bootstrapping procedure for selecting the training samples.

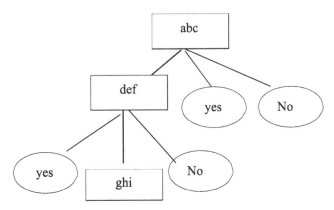

Fig. 5. Decision tree for training with classes yes and no

3.4 Support Vector Machine

It is a powerful classification algorithm construct a straight line that separates two classes apart. To construct a hyperplane first we have to transform the dimensional into vectors. The optimal hyperplane is constructed by (Cortes and Vapnik 1995). The hyperplane maximizes the features in dataset and identify the possible distance for optimal hyperplane

$$W_0 \cdot x + b_0 = 0 \tag{1}$$

The W_0 is the normal vector of the hyperplane, b is the scalar and x is the vector of the input vector. When the optimal hyperplane is found the data line lie in that plane. That means complexity cannot affect the features and number of training of instances.

3.5 Logistic Regression

It is the statistical technique widely used for analyzing relationship between variables with categorical outcome. It aimed at finding the best fitting model. Logistic regression (Diviya Prabha and Ratthipriya 2018) was chosen because the predicted variable is categorical (either admitted or not admitted). The Logistic regression is given by

$$= \begin{cases} 0 & \textit{Patient is not readmitted} \\ 1 & \textit{Patient is readmitted} \end{cases} \quad i = 1, 2, \ldots n$$

$$p = \frac{1}{1 + e^{-(\beta_0 + \beta_1 x_1 + \beta_2 x_2 \cdots)}}$$

Where idp_i symbolizes independent variables, signifies dependent variables, p is the probability of independent variables, is coefficient of constant term, the $\pi(idp_i)$ is the probability of patient readmitted depends on p-independent variables in the dataset. x_1 x_2 also represents independent variables.

Table 3. Accuracy prediction for machine learning techniques

S. No	Machine learning algorithm	Accuracy	RMSE
1)	Logistic Regression	95%	0.25
2)	Decision Tree	93%	0.30
3)	Random Forest	92%	0.32
4)	SVM	90%	0.40

The above Table 3 describes the machine learning techniques with accuracy score and root mean square value from the table it justifies that logistic regression provides high accuracy when compared with other models and similarly the Root Mean Square Error (RMSE) is minimum for logistic regression. The formula is calculates ads [15]

$$RMSE = \sqrt{\frac{1}{n}\sum_{i=1}^{n}(C_i - T_i)^2}$$

Where C_i is the predicted value for readmission and T_i is the target value of readmission. N represents number of training samples. Hyper parameters is the method of ability to learn make a model. Choosing the correct parameter is an important task in machine learning which will avoid over fitting. It is helps to choose the best features that support for predictability.

The Table 4 describes the logistic regression model to the dependent variable. It exemplifies true positive rate of the model, false positive rate, true negative and false negative rate with classification accuracy of 95%. To improve the accuracy a new approach ensemble method is carried on tuning the hyperparameter. Three methods are chosen to optimize the parameter and improve the prediction accuracy. Learning hyperparameter is difficult than that of training it. The best method is chosen based on prediction accuracy. The three methods are:

- Randomized
- Correlation
- Entropy

a)   Randomized Hyper parameter Tuning Logistic Regression (RHTLR)

Table 4. Classification table for logistic regression

Observed	Predicted		Accuracy (%)
	True	False	
Positive	21341	1983	95
Negative	226	6716	

The model chooses any two parameters randomly and starts to run the model. Among the 11 variables any two are features are selected randomly and their parameter are tuned. It choose the optimal parameter to make the model an efficient one. The main disadvantage of this method is as the feature is selected randomly the most significant features for the prediction are missed. So the prediction accuracy is same when the model is run. The random features are inefficient for target class. While tuning random numbers there is no difference in prediction value.

a) Correlation Based Hyperparameter Tuning Logistic Regression (CBHTLR)

This model chooses two parameters that have high relationship with the target variable readmitted. It expresses the relationship with the value of the variables and the taken to the consideration. While tuning the parameter with the correlated value the prediction value is increased slightly but there is no much effective for prediction.

b) Entropy Based Hyper parameter Tuning Logistic Regression (EBHTLR)

Entropy is the measure of randomness or uncertainty from the features that is to be processed. The values which are lower those features is taken for parameter tuning. That is if the entropy value is low then its predictability is high for the occurrence. The aim is to reduce uncertainty. From the Table 2 the entropy value for least four features are taken their parameter values are tuned. The formula for entropy is given below

$$\text{ENTROPY} = \sum_{i=1}^{n} -p_i \log_2 p_i$$

Where the probability for each features is are calculated from dataset after performing logistic regression. Those features with low entropy have high accuracy of prediction for parameter tuning. Figure 6 depicts the plotted graph of entropy and correlation value for parameter tuning.

```
Algorithm: BHTLR
BEGIN D: Features ,S: Data Set
START
# Feature Selection
        Best FS_D(S):
            If Features (D) = max (entropy (features (D)) else
            Delete Features_D End If
#Readmission Prediction
    Prediction _LR (Features_info):
        For each Features_info in S
        LR= Logistic Regression ()
        End For
#Parameter Tuning
        Perform Parameter tuning (Random) Calculate
        Entropy:
                For each Features_info in S
                Entropy = min (Entropy (Features info))
        End For
        Update Parameter tuning (Entropy)
END
```

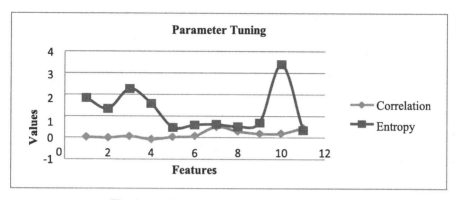

Fig. 6. Entropy and correlation values for features

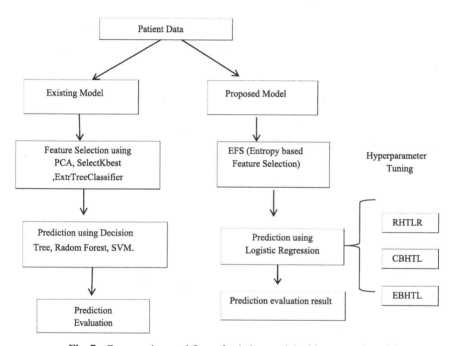

Fig. 7. Comparative workflow of existing model with proposed model

Figure 7 explains the comparative workflow of existing approach and proposed approach. The patient data is carried out in two approach exiting approach for feature selection using the methods PCA, SelectKbest and Extra Tree Classifier. After feature selection readmission prediction using machine learning techniques such as Decision Tree, Random Forest and SVM is its evaluation results are calculated using metrics such as precision, recall and f1 measure. The proposed approach for feature selection using entropy which is the EFS method and prediction using logistic regression is performed an ensemble methods are used to improve the prediction accuracy. The three methods

RHTLR, CBHTL and EBHTL are used for hyper parameter tuning. The prediction evaluations are carried out for the proposed approach which is comparatively better accuracy than existing approach. The algorithm describes the prediction model of the proposed work three steps are followed to make the algorithm an effective method Step 1 is the feature selection that are performed using entropy. Step 2 is the prediction model of various machine learning techniques the logistic regression techniques that is improved in accuracy level is taken for hyperparameter tuning to improve the accuracy level. Step 3 describes three methods are followed for tuning randomized method which is the default method, second is correlation method and entropy method. From these methods three feature values are taken for tuning the model. The entropy based model improves the accuracy than the existing method.

4   Results and Discussions

To identify the significant of proposed approach the evaluation is required. The performance of the model is mainly under the perspective of classification accuracy and running time. Pyspark environment helps the machine to run in parallel.

The Table 5 exemplifies the probability of the predicted values it is shown that the values of the proposed model are consequently increasing and it is also high when compared to the other model. Logistic Regression has outperformed well for the parallel framework and less computation time. The values are calculated for 13 iteration and the result is obtained to the table.

Table 5. Probability of predicted values

Iteration	Decision Tree	Random Forest	GBT	EBHTLG
1	0.69	0.92	0.89	0.93
2	0.67	0.92	0.87	0.92
3	0.75	0.79	0.93	0.96
4	0.79	0.87	0.93	0.95
5	0.78	0.84	0.93	0.96
6	0.76	0.8	0.93	0.95
7	0.78	0.84	0.93	0.95
8	0.9	0.88	0.93	0.96
9	0.79	0.88	0.93	0.93
10	0.79	0.88	0.93	0.96
11	0.78	0.84	0.93	0.96
12	0.79	0.88	0.93	0.88
13	0.75	0.83	0.83	0.89

The Table 4 designates the statistics of each model such as precision, recall, F1-Score and weighted precision, weighted recall, weighted F1-Score. It also illuminates the False Positive Rate from which concludes that EBHTLR performs the best model among the other model (Table 6).

Table 6. Performance of each model Statistic

Classification algorithm	Precision	Recall	F1-Score	w-Precision	w-Recall	W F1-Score	FPR
Decision Tree	0.8963	0.886	0.891	0.92	0.89	0.91	0.04
Random Forest	0.9043	0.904	0.904	0.90	0.86	0.90	0.04
GBT Classifier	0.9054	0.905	0.905	0.90	0.90	0.90	0.04
RHTLR	0.9123	0.903	0.907	0.91	0.90	0.91	0.03
CBHTLR	0.9145	0.914	0.914	0.90	0.90	0.90	0.03
EBHTLR	0.9234	0.923	0.923	0.93	0.91	0.92	0.02

Table 7 reveals the accuracy of the model that is chosen for hyper parameter tuning. Among the three methods EBHTLR performs better accuracy.

Table 7. Accuracy for hyper parameter tuning model

Hyperparameter tuning models	Accuracy (%)
RHTLR	95.23
CBHTLR	95.45
EBHTLR	96.42

5   Conclusion

In this proposed work, an efficient pyspark process EBHTLR approach was implemented for readmission prediction. Feature selection EFS technique was used to identify the best features. Through, evaluation it is proved that proposed model is scalable for computing large dataset. The prediction accuracy is also high compared to other models. This model is effective and improves patient care.

References

Lacson, R.C., Baker, B., Suresh, H.: Use of machine-learning algorithms to determine features of systolic blood pressure variability that predict poor outcomes in hypertensive patient. Clin. Kidney J. **12**(2), 206–212 (2019)

Cai, J., Luo, J.: Feature selection in machine learning: a new perspective. J. NeuroComput. **300**, 70–79 (2018)

Cortes, C., Vapnik, V.: Support-vector network. Mach. Learn. **20**, 273–297 (1995). https://doi.org/10.1007/BF00994018

Diviya Prabha, V., Ratthipriya, R.: Prediction of hyperglycemia using binary gravitational logistic regression (BGLR). J. Pure Appl. Math. **118**(16), 105–119 (2018)

Hammoudeh, A., Al-Naymat, G., Ghannam, I., Obied, N.: Predicting hospital readmission among diabetics using deep learning. Procedia Comput. Sci. **141**, 484–489 (2018)

Jayanthi, N., Babu, B.Vijaya, Sambasiva Rao, N.: Survey on clinical prediction models for diabetes prediction. J. Big Data **4**(1), 1–15 (2017). https://doi.org/10.1186/s40537-017-0082-7

Wang, L., Ann, C.: Big data analytics for medication management in diabetes mellitus. Int. J. Stud. Nurs. **1**(1), 42–55 (2016)

Louppe, G., Wehenkel, L., Sutera, A., Geurts, P.: Understanding variable importances in forests of randomized trees. In: Advances in neural information processing systems (n.d.)

Islam, M.S., Hasan, M.M., Wang, X., Germack, H.D.: A systematic review on healthcare analytics: application and theoretical perspective of data mining. In: Healthcare, vol. 6, no (2), p. 54 (2018)

Mingle, D.: Predicting diabetic readmission rates: moving beyond Hba1c. Curr. Trends Biomed. Eng. Biosci. **7**(3), 555707 (2017)

Moon, M., Lee, S.K.: Applying of decision tree analysis to risk factors associated with pressure ulcers in long-term care facilities. Healthc. Inf. Res. Korean Soc. Med. Inf. **23**(1), 43–52 (2017)

Quinlan, J.R.: Induction of decision trees. Mach. Learn. **1**, 81–106 (1986). https://doi.org/10.1007/BF00116251

Brindise, L.R., Steele, R.J.: Machine learning-based pre-discharge prediction of hospital readmission. In: 2018 International Conference on Computer, Information and Telecommunication Systems (CITS), pp. 1–5. IEEE (2018)

Sneha, N., Gangil, T.: Analysis of diabetes mellitus for early prediction using optimal features selection. J. Big Data **6**(1), 1–19 (2019). https://doi.org/10.1186/s40537-019-0175-6

Tashkandia, A., Wiesea, I., Wiese, L.: Efficient in-database patient similarity analysis for personalized medical decision support systems. Preprint submitted to Elsevier (2018)

Yifan, X., Sharma, J.: Diabetes patient readmission prediction using big data analytic tools, pp. 1–30 (2014)

Cyber Security

An Evaluation of Convolutional Neural Networks for Malware Family Classification

Shreya Davis[(✉)], C. N. Sminesh[(✉)], K. S. Akshay[(✉)], T. R. Akshay[(✉)],
and Anjali Ranjith[(✉)]

Government Engineering College, Thrissur, India
shreya.davis1996@gmail.com, smineshcn@gectcr.ac.in, akshayks3573@gmail.com,
akshaytrajesh@gmail.com, anjaliranjith97@gmail.com

Abstract. There has been a rapid rise and diversification in the quantity and types of malware that are currently being propagated. Hence, the need for a proper mechanism to classify these different types of malware are of paramount importance. Academic researchers have been analysing malware samples to understand how they behave and they study the techniques used by malware developers to improve the security of the existing infrastructure. Malware analysis can be used for both the detection of malware and malware classification. In this work, modern convolutional neural networks (CNN) are evaluated for the task of malware classification using image data. The networks that are used for testing are, VGG, ResNet, Inception-V3, and Xception. These networks have proven to work with high performance on huge ImageNet dataset, but the possibility of using such CNN's needs to be checked for the very specific task of malware classification. Comparing the results, Xception Network provided the best performance with an accuracy of 99% and proved to be the fastest network. In terms of training Inception Network was better. Furthermore, individual precision and recall values were calculated for each family.

Keywords: Malware classification · Convolutional neural network · ResNet · Inception-V3 · Xception · VGG

1 Introduction

The Internet has various applications like doing transactions, communication, entertainment, e-shopping, and various other commercial and non-commercial activities. Even though it makes our life convenient, the Internet has made us vulnerable to external threats. Illegitimate users commit financial fraud or steal private and sensitive information from legitimate users using malware programs. The number of such reported malware attacks is increasing with every passing year.

Malware is malevolent software that is intentionally designed to induce a threat to the security of the system or to infiltrate without the user's consent.

© Springer Nature Singapore Pte Ltd. 2020
S. Balusamy et al. (Eds.): ICC3 2019, CCIS 1213, pp. 51–60, 2020.
https://doi.org/10.1007/978-981-15-9700-8_5

They can be of different forms such as an executable, HTML file, etc. Malware developers use such illicit programs to do social engineering attacks like phishing, create bots, install backdoors and get root access. Most attacks involve the implementation of malicious software. The Emotnet attack and WannaCry Ransomware attack, to name a few. The complexity of these attacks also keeps increasing with the rise of digital footprint.

Recent advances in parallel processing libraries and hardware design have made it possible to utilize deep neural networks for real-time image classification. Convolutional neural networks are a class of deep learning neural networks that analyze deep visual imagery.

Visualization provides a means of getting a comprehensive view of any system or data. Images or pictorial representation makes more sense than any other kind of representation. In this case, visual representation is generated for a binary file and that generated representation is used to examine the patterns visible in it. These are then used for the classification of the given malware file to its family. Classification of malware into its respective family helps an analyst to get a better understanding of the details regarding the functioning of the malware. Malware samples with a similar code structure are grouped into one class. This in turn helps to have an insight on devising sanitation and detection techniques. This also helps in devising a general idea about the behavior if we know the family to which the malware belongs.

In the above section, an introduction to malware analysis and classification is discussed. In Sect. 2, literature survey conducted as part of the experiment is discussed along with the convolutional neural networks used in the experiment. In Sect. 3, the proposed method and the obtained results for each model are discussed. And the conclusion section is given in Sect. 4.

2   Literature Survey

In this work, a detailed literature survey has been conducted on different techniques for malware classification and deep learning. The details are given in the following section.

2.1   Malware Visualisation Approaches

Helfman [3] applied the dot plot data visualisation technique to software programs and by his technique, he showed that visualisation helps in the identification of software design patterns. In his technique, first, the data is tokenized. Then the rows and columns are labelled by a sequence of tokens. A Graph is plotted such that a dot is plotted if the tokens match and a blank is plotted if they don't. The graph thus obtained will always be symmetrical.

Conti et al. [4] used an automated binary mapping technique. He used Byte plot visualisation technique for files with little or no knowledge about the file format. His work showed that carefully crafted visualizations provide a bigger picture and facilitate rapid analysis of both medium and large binary files.

Nataraj et al. [2] were the first in devising the method for automatic malware classification using byte plot visualisation. They found that for many malware families, the images belonging to the same family appear very similar in layout and texture. In their method, malware samples were converted to greyscale byte plot representations. The resultant image is then used to extract texture based features. For computing texture features from images, they used GIST, which is an abstract representation technique.

Han et al. [5] proposed a method to visually analyze malware by transforming malware binary information into image matrices. Their method is divided into three steps. In Step 1, binary information is extracted from binary sample files. Step 2 involves generation of image matrices in which the binary information is recorded as RGB colored pixels. In Step 3, the similarities between the image matrices are calculated through selective area matching.

All the above methods use visualization approaches for malware classification. There are also other methods that classify malware using statistical or dynamic analysis like malware detection using process behaviour [12], using pattern matching techniques [13], using analysis of malware executables [14], and using malware signatures [15].

2.2 Convolutional Neural Networks

A Convolution Neural Network (CNN) is a feed-forward neural network. CNN is the current state-of-the-art neural network architecture for image classification problems. CNN is comprised of neurons with learnable weights and biases. Many types of CNN's have been used by researchers in the past (LeNet-5); however, the recent ones with more efficiency were chosen for the evaluation.

ResNet. For the comparison purpose ResNet50 - ResNet with 50 layers is chosen. The Resnet network [6] has residual building blocks that solve the problem of training and testing errors in plain networks on going deep. Usually, neural networks learn features at the end of several layers, but in resnet, we are trying to learn the residues. As we add layers to the neural network it is observed that the training accuracy goes down, this is known as the degradation problem. This inability of neural networks stemmed because learning from identity mapping was becoming laborious. There exists a solution to the deeper model by adding additional layers called identity mapping and copying the other layers from the already learned shallower model. This stops the new solution from having a higher training error than the learned shallower model.

ResNet50 requires only 3.8 billion floating point operations (FLOP).

VGG-19. In 2014, The VGG network went deeper than its competitors and could have up to 19 layers. The network [7] was invented by Simonyan and Zisserman and the network could classify images to up to 1000 different object categories.

The network is trained on a huge dataset from the ImageNet database. Owing to the usage of small receptive fields, the network goes deep, which leads to better generalization. This network is simple and uses only 3×3 convolutional layers which are stacked on top of each other in increasing depth. For a given receptive field, which is the effective area size of the input image on which the output depends, multiple stacked small size kernels are used instead of a large kernel. Doing so increases the depth of the network and thus the model can learn more complex features at a lower cost.

Inception. This type of network [8] architecture uses a new approach in which along with stacked layers like those in traditional neural networks, layers also run parallel to each other.

The parallel modules are called Inception modules. These Inception modules helped in limiting the number of parameters and at the same time increase the total number of layers considerably.

Layer with a 5×5 connection can be replaced with two 3×3 layers that help in achieving a small number of parameters. Doing so also reduces the computation necessary as 5×5 is more expensive than the 3×3 layers.

Further reduction in computation can be achieved by replacing the 3×3 layer by 3 3×1 output layers. The network thus obtained is the Inception V3 network. The next version Inception V4 has a more simplified architecture with better performance due to the increased number of inception layers.

Xception. The Xception network [9] is the extreme version of the Inception network obtained by using convolutions which are depthwise separable by maximizing the number of towers in a module. The number of parameters for the Xception network is the same as the Inception V3 network. But at the same time, the performance of the Xception network was better than the Inception network.

3   The Proposed System Architecture

The diagram given below shows the Proposed model used for comparison in this paper. The reason for selecting this model is its significant accuracy in small interval of time. Furthermore, there is no need for executing the malware which reduces the vulnerability of system where analysis is taking place (Fig. 1).

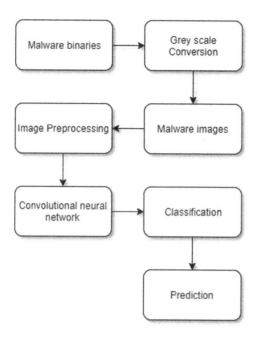

Fig. 1. Proposed system architecture

4   Experiments and Results

The dataset used for this paper, the networks used, training the models, the final results obtained and the observations made are given below.

4.1   DataSet

For the purpose of this paper, a standard dataset comprising grayscale images of the respective malwares are used. The dataset used is the malimg dataset. It consists of 9339 samples from 25 malware families, ranging from 80 to 200 samples per family. From the given malware binary which is read as a vector consisting of 8 bits unsigned integers, a 2D array is obtained. These 8 bit integer is mapped to a range [0, 255] (0: black, 255: white) and the binary is visualized as a grayscale image. The image width is fixed to be 256 and image height vary depending on the malware executable. The following table shows malware variants.

4.2   Model Training

To evaluate the proposed model performance, stratified 10-fold cross-validation [10] is used. In this method, the samples are randomly partitioned into ten disjoint sets of equal size. Each set roughly contains the same proportions of the

Family	Number of samples
Adialer.C	122
Agent.FYI	116
Allaple.A	2949
Allaple.L	1591
Alueron.gen!J	198
Autorun.K	106
C2LOP.gen!g	200
C2LOP.P	146
Dialplatform.B	177
Dontovo.A	162
Fakerean	381
Instantaccess	431
Lolyda.AA1	213
Lolyda.AA2	184
Lolyda.AA3	123
Lolyda.AT	159
Malex.gen!J	136
Obfuscator.AD	142
Rbot!gen	158
Skintrim.N	80
Swizzor.gen!E	128
Swizzor.gen!I	132
VB.AT	408
Wintrim.BX	97
Yuner.A	800

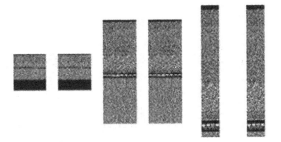

Fig. 2. Sample grayscale images of different malware families

class labels in each fold. One set is selected as the testing set and all the other sets as the training set. This process is repeated 10 times selecting each partition as testing set. The average classification accuracy, loss and execution time are calculated for each fold (Fig. 2).

Training parameters were kept equal and Adam equalizer [11] was used for all neural networks to compare CNN's. The number of epochs was set to 10 and the batch size was given as 64. The data were pre-processed and labeled before using it to train different models.

4.3 Experimental Results

The four different networks require different training time to train the same dataset due to the varying complexity of the networks. Training time taken by each network for a single epoch is given in the table below.

Model	Average accuracy	Test accuracy
ResNet50	0.9630	0.9947
VGG19	0.2723	0.3189
Inception	0.9637	0.9828
Xception	0.9908	0.9946

Model	Time for the first epoch (in s)
ResNet50	8698.0079
VGG19	11513.2786
Inception	6783.2548
Xception	12544.2458

The accuracy was calculated for each model and noted in the table. The accuracy is calculated using the equation:

$$accuracy = \frac{TP + TN}{P + N};$$

where P+N is given by TP+TN+FP+FN TP denotes True Positives, TN true negatives, FP is false positives and FN is false negatives. Recall and precison are calculated by the equations:

$$recall = \frac{TP}{TP + FN}$$

$$precision = \frac{TP}{TP + FN}$$

Analyzing the test results, the average accuracy for VGG-19 is 27.23% and test accuracy of 31.89%. It had a precision of 2% and recall of 4.16% and was only able to classify two malware families, as vgg-19 requires a lot of sample data for accurate classification. Only two malware categories had more that

1000 samples, Allaple.A and Allaple.L. Hence it showed predictions only for the above two. Due to its greater depth it is painfully slow to train and apparently least effective compared to the other models.

The average accuracy for Resnet is 96.30% and test accuracy is 99.47%. It had a precision of 94.92% and recall of 94%. It turned out to be comparatively easier to train as it was fast and model size was also smaller.

The average accuracy for Inception is 96.37% and test accuracy of 98.28%. It had a precision of 90.48% and recall of 92%. The fastest to train with least size.

The best performance is of the Xception network which gave an average accuracy of 99.08% and a test accuracy of 99.46%. It had a precision of 97.4% and recall of 97.6%.

Family	Resnet50		VGG19		Inception		Xception	
	Precision	Recall	Precision	Recall	Precision	Recall	Precision	Recall
Adialer.C	0.97	1	0	0	0.99	1	1	1
Agent.FYI	1	0.99	0	0	1	1	1	1
Allaple.A	0.99	0.95	0.31	0.7	0.99	0.99	0.99	1
Allaple.L	0.91	1	0.17	0.3	0.99	1	1	1
Alueron.gen!J	1	0.96	0	0	1	0.99	0.99	1
Autorun.K	0.99	0.9	0	0	0	0	1	1
C2LOP.gen!g	0.9	0.9	0	0	0.95	0.89	0.95	0.98
C2LOP.P	0.77	0.84	0	0	0.82	0.9	0.92	0.9
Dialplatform.B	0.98	0.99	0	0	0.99	1	1	1
Dontovo.A	0.99	1	0	0	1	1	1	1
Fakerean	0.97	0.98	0	0	0.78	0.99	0.99	0.99
Instantaccess	1	1	0	0	0.99	1	1	1
Lolyda.AA1	0.97	0.97	0	0	0.95	1	0.98	1
Lolyda.AA2	0.96	0.98	0	0	0.99	0.96	1	0.99
Lolyda.AA3	0.99	0.99	0	0	0.99	0.99	1	0.99
Lolyda.AT	0.97	0.96	0	0	1	0.99	0.99	0.99
Malex.gen!J	0.99	0.88	0	0	0.93	0.99	0.99	0.99
Obfuscator.AD	1	1	0	0	1	0.92	0.99	1
Rbot!gen	0.94	1	0	0	1	0.99	1	1
Skintrim.N	0.98	1	0	0	0.97	0.98	1	1
Swizzor.gen!E	0.81	0.63	0	0	0.8	0.77	0.82	0.78
Swizzor.gen!I	0.68	0.79	0	0	0.75	0.78	0.75	0.8
VB.AT	0.99	0.99	0	0	0.99	1	0.99	0.99
Wintrim.BX	1	0.8	0	0	0.87	0.97	1	1
Yuner.A	0.98	1	0	0	0.88	0.9	1	1

5   Conclusion

In this paper, analysis was done on different convolutional neural networks using malware images and predicting the malware family of a malware file by converting the executable into an image. The techniques used and findings from each network were noted. Each network took varying time and showed varying accuracy. The Xception network was found best suited for the classification with an accuracy of 99%.Vgg-19 proved the least efficient with 27 % accuracy as it required a significant amount of samples for classification and hence was able to classify only Allaple families which had more than 1500 samples. Resnet and Inception were easier to train and had comparable accuracies. For future work, the malware samples in each of the family could be increased for better analysis.

References

1. Singh, A., Handa, A., Kumar, N., Shukla, S.K.: Malware classification using image representation. In: Dolev, S., Hendler, D., Lodha, S., Yung, M. (eds.) CSCML 2019. LNCS, vol. 11527, pp. 75–92. Springer, Cham (2019). https://doi.org/10.1007/978-3-030-20951-3_6

2. Nataraj, L., Karthikeyan, S., Jacob, G., Manjunath, B.: Malware images: visualization and automatic classification. In: Proceedings of the 8th International Symposium on Visualization for Cyber Security (2011). https://doi.org/10.1145/2016904.2016908

3. Helfman, J.: Dotplot patterns: a literal look at pattern languages. TAPOS **2**, 31–41 (1996)

4. Conti, G., Bratus, S., Shubina, A., Sangster, B., Ragsdale, R., Supan, M., Lichtenberg, A., Perez-Alemany, R.: Automated mapping of large binary objects using primitive fragmenttype classification. Digital Invest. (2010). https://doi.org/10.1016/j.diin.2010.05.002

5. Han, K., Lim, J., Im, E.G.: Malware analysis method using visualization of binary files. In: Proceedings of the 2013 Research in Adaptive and Convergent Systems, RACS 2013, pp. 317–321 (2013). https://doi.org/10.1145/2513228.2513294

6. Gajic, B., Vazquez, E., Baldrich, R.: Evaluation of deep image descriptors for texture retrieval. In: Proceedings of the 12th International Joint Conference on Computer Vision, Imaging and Computer Graphics Theory and Applications - Volume 5: VISAPP, (VISIGRAPP 2017), pp. 251-257 (2017). https://doi.org/10.5220/0006129302510257. ISBN 978-989-758-226-4

7. Liu, S., Deng, W.: Very deep convolutional neural network based image classification using small training sample size. In: 2015 3rd IAPR Asian Conference on Pattern Recognition (ACPR), pp. 730–734 (2015)

8. Szegedy, C., et al.: Going deeper with convolutions. In: 2015 IEEE Conference on Computer Vision and Pattern Recognition (CVPR), Boston, MA, pp. 1–9 (2015). https://doi.org/10.1109/CVPR.2015.7298594

9. Chollet, F.: Xception: deep learning with depthwise separable convolutions. In: 2017 IEEE Conference on Computer Vision and Pattern Recognition (CVPR), pp. 1800–1807 (2016)

10. Kohavi, R.: A study of cross-validation and bootstrap for accuracy estimation and model selection, vol. 14 (2001)

11. Kingma, D.P., Ba, J.: Adam: a method for stochastic optimization. In: International Conference on Learning Representations (2014)

12. Tobiyama, S., et al.: Malware detection with deep neural network using process behavior. In: 2016 IEEE 40th Annual Computer Software and Applications Conference (COMPSAC), vol. 2, pp. 577–582 (2016)

13. Sahu, M.K., Ahirwar, M., Hemlata, A.: A review of malware detection based on pattern matching technique. Int. J. Comput. Sci. Inf. Technol. (IJCSIT) **5**(1), 944–947 (2014)

14. Masud, M., Khan, L., Thuraisingham, B.: A hybrid model to detect malicious executables. In: 2007 IEEE International Conference on Communications, pp. 1443–1448 (2007). https://doi.org/10.1109/ICC.2007.242

15. Abou-Assaleh, T., Cercone, N., Keselj, V., Sweidan, R.: Detection of new malicious code using N-grams signatures. In: PST, pp. 193–196 (2004)

An Exploration of Changes Addressed in the Android Malware Detection Walkways

Rincy Raphael[1(✉)] and P. Mathiyalagan[2]

[1] Anna University, Chennai, India
rincyraphael2012@gmail.com
[2] Sri Ramakrishna Engineering College, Coimbatore, India
p_mathi2001@yahoo.co.in

Abstract. Smartphone users are increasing rapidly because of the convenience and flexibility available with smartphones. Most of the digital transactions are performed using this simple hand-held device. Android is the evergreen platform for mobile operating system. The availability of applications is the main attraction for both legitimate users as well as the vulnerability injectors. Malware is malicious software perpetrators dispatch to infect individual mobile devices. It exploits target system vulnerabilities, such as a bug in legitimate android applications that can be hijacked for malicious activities. Various machine learning approaches are applied to classify the Android Malwares from the goodwares. This paper studied the existing framework for android malware detection techniques such as signature, anomaly and topic modelling based. The proposed methods also evaluated with system accuracy, analysis types and benefits and limitations of each proposed frameworks.

Keywords: Android malware · Data mining approaches · Machine learning · Topic modeling

1 Introduction

A smartphone is a small mobile device that can do more than other traditional cellular phones and work as like a computer. The portability, efficiency, accuracy in digitalized banking transactions and other attractive features in the smartphone are all time steals the heart of even the normal users. The smartphone user's number has reached 2.3 billion at the end of 2017 and now it is reached at 2.7 billion in beginning of 2019 [1]. Android is one of the mobile operating system, based upon a modified version of the Linux kernel [8]. Most of the smartphone manufacture make use of the android platform which having the feasibility to support different applications that can increase the functionality of the mobile devices. The smartphone manufacturers have seen Android as an opportunity to turn the current users keen interest for this open source OS into a way to win market share. As per the report of Mobile Operating System Market Share Worldwide, 76.03% of Market Share held by the Android platform [2]. Hence Android has become one of the most valuable targets for malware developers where are more than

© Springer Nature Singapore Pte Ltd. 2020
S. Balusamy et al. (Eds.): ICC3 2019, CCIS 1213, pp. 61–84, 2020.
https://doi.org/10.1007/978-981-15-9700-8_6

500 different Android markets that may contain malicious applications that can infect the Android platform by propagating through various App-stores as well as Android devices. Most of the malware writers focus on third party markets to distribute infected applications to earn profit. It became easy to steal users credential information and make them to do unnecessary activities. Android malware include Phishing, Banking-Trojans, Spyware, Bots, Root Exploits, SMS Fraud, Premium Dialers and Fake Installers [3]. These malwares are mainly distributed in markets operated by third parties, but even the Google Android Market cannot guarantee that all of its listed applications are threat free. Banking malwares are one of the agitated abuses that can enter our devices by exploiting known security vulnerabilities. In first quadrant of 2019, Kaspersky Lab products and technologies detected that 905,174 malicious installation packages, 29,841 new mobile banking Trojans and 27,928 new mobile ransomware Trojans [5]. The Google play store contains 2,726,158 android apps where 13% of the considered to be low quality apps in 2019 [6]. The results show that the efficient and effective mechanism is needed to solve the problem.

The lacks of security features in android platform inspires the 98% of attacker to steal users credential by launching malicious applications in devices with android based mobile operating system [7]. Various machine learning techniques [13] are already proposed to mitigate the attacks in the android platform. Signature based methods are failed in the "zero day attacks" whereas time consumption is a problem in behaviour based methods. Hence it is need to have access to a scalable solution for quickly analysing new apps and identifying and isolating malicious applications. This paper is studying the efficiency and accuracy of existing signature, behavioural as well as the latest topic model techniques to analysis the android malwares.

2   Android Based Malware Detection Techniques

Malware Detection can be performed by various approaches such as Signature based, Anomaly or Behavioural based and most modern Topic Modeling based. After extracting the features, Machine learning algorithms are applied for filtering the most significant features to classify the android Apk samples [14] as malware or benign. Naives Bayes (NB), Decision Tree (DT), RandomForest (RF), J48, Support Vector Machine (SVM), Multilayer Perceptron (MLP), K-mean, K-Nearest Neighbours (KNN), Artificial Neural Networks (ANN), Neuro fuzzy etc. are the wide range of supervised and unsupervised machine learning methods exist for the malware study (Refer Fig. 1).

2.1   Signature Based

Most malware detection methods are based on traditional content signature based approaches in which they use a list of malware signature definitions, and compare each application against the database of known malware signatures. Signature-based malware detection technology is mainly used in Antivirus programs where the malicious signature is already known and available in the database. The systematic way of signature based method is shown in Fig. 2.

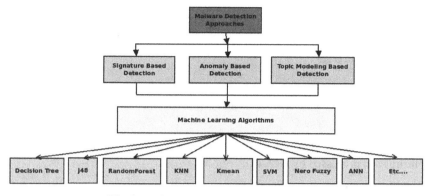

Fig. 1. Various malware detection approaches

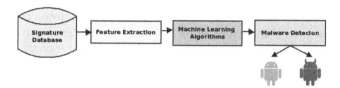

Fig. 2. Malware detection using signature based approach

The disadvantage of this detection method is that users are only protected from malware that are detected by most recently updated signatures, but not protected from new malware (i.e. zero-day attack). Also, it's very expensive process because it requires a large collection of dataset with frequently updated malware signature, which leads to increase in processing time as well as storage space.

2.2 Anomaly Based

Anomaly or Behavioural based malware detection evaluates an object based on its intended actions before it can actually execute that behaviour. An object's behaviour, or in some cases its potential behaviour, is analysed for suspicious activities. Attempts to perform actions that are clearly abnormal or unauthorized would indicate the object is malicious, or at least suspicious. There's a multitude of behaviours that point to potential danger. Some examples include any attempt to discover a sandbox environment, disabling security controls, installing rootkits, and registering for auto start. Evaluating for malicious behaviour as it executes is called dynamic analysis. Threat potential or malicious intent can also be assessed by static analysis, which looks for dangerous capabilities within the object's code and structure [10]. The Fig. 3 explains the Anomaly based malware detection technique.

Behaviour based approaches also exhibits some disadvantages. Conventional sandbox technologies have limited visibility and can only evaluate the interaction between an object and the operating system. By observing 100% of the actions that a malicious object might take, even when it delegates those actions to the operating system or other

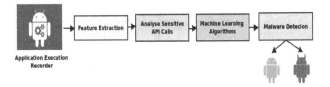

Fig. 3. Malware detection anomaly or behavioural based approach

programs, CSOs can evaluate not only the malware communication with the OS, but each instruction processed by the CPU.

2.3 Topic Modeling Based

Machine Learning approaches are widely accepted for android malware detection. At the same time, the source codes of the android applications are not always compared with the implemented android app behaviour for malware detection. To effectively solve this problem, Topic modeling techniques are used to extract the text features from the app description, reviews and user recommendations. The extracted text feature informations are used for classifying the malware (Refer Fig. 4).

Fig. 4. Malware detection using topic modeling based approach

3   Review of Literature

The review is conducted on only the selected studies according to existing methodologies and discussed the cons and pros for the various proposed systems.

3.1   Signature Based Approaches

Lichao Sun et al. [15] introduced a malware detection system SIGPID to analyse the significant permissions using the multi-level pruning technique. Dataset is designed by 178 malicious app families and randomly downloaded benign apps from Google play store as single family. The most relevant 22 permissions out of 135 were identified and Support Vector Machine (SVM) is used as the classifier. The detection rate of known and unknown malware is 93.62% and 91.4% respectively. SIGPID achieved detection accuracy by 90% as well as the runtime performance improved by 85.6%. As compared with the previous anti-virus systems, the SIGPIG is efficiently classified the known and unknown malwares in a systematic way - through 3-level pruning approach.

Santos I et al. [16] proposed a signature model based on the frequency of the appearance of opcode sequences and provided an empirical validation that the method is capable of detecting unknown malware. The 17000 malware samples were taken from the VxHeavens website and 1000 legitimate executable were from the author's personal choice. Top 1000 features were selected, which represents the 0.6% of the total number of features extracted using Information Gain algorithm. Instance Selection (IS) and Feature Selection (FS) are very effective at reducing the size of the training set and helping to filtrate and clean noisy data. Various classifiers are implemented with the help of machine learning tool WEKA, such as Decision tree, K-nearest neighbour, Bayesian Networks and SVM with detection rate for opcodes length n = 1 is 91:43, 92:83 90:65 and 92:92 respectively. Similarly, detection rate for an opcode-sequence length of n = 2 is 95:26, 94:83, 93:40 and 95:90 respectively for the same data mining classifiers.

Cui et al. [17] implemented a novel recognition framework of both combining the cloud environment and packet examination techniques. The proposed framework identifies the malicious mobile malware behaviour with the utilization of data mining strategies. This approach totally keeps away from the distortion of traditional techniques. The framework with special governance is arranged and can be sent by portable administrators to send alertness to clients who have malware on their utensil. The withdrawal grouping method is suggested to enhance the execution of proposed model. This technique utilizes earlier learning to lessen dataset measure. Additionally, a multi-module location plan was acquainted with improve framework precision. The system is incorporating the location consequences of a few operations, including Naive Bayes and Decision Tree, to provide the better results as compare to the customary methods.

Yujie Fan et al. [18] developed a data mining based detection frame work called Malicious Sequential Pattern based Malware Detection (MSPMD), which is composed of the proposed sequential pattern mining algorithm (MSPE) and All-Nearest-Neighbor (ANN) classifier. The use of designed filtering criterion as well as the deployment of detection module with new nearest classifiers makes the framework more systematic from conventional models. The recommended model attained accuracy of 93.40% and 95.25% respectively with Intelligence Malware Detection System (IMDS) and MSPMD detection systems. Their structure beats other to exchange knowledge mining based discovery techniques in distinguishing new revengeful attacking executable.

Wu et al. [19] implemented a hybrid approach with an artificial immune-based smartphone malware detection model (SP-MDM). As like the classical artificial immune model, the proposed framework investigated the malware in the android platform. In the proposed model, the static and dynamic marks of malware are separated and the antigens are produced by the intelligent venerated vector encoding mechanism. Gene Pool management used to discover new genes that can be perceived abnormal behaviour whereas Immature Detector Detect used to convert the memory detector for rapid detection of malware with the alarm signal and to find the sufficient number of antigens within the prescribed time else the detector will be erase the data. The artificial immune based model attained 87.7% detection rate with test set held twenty number malware as well as benign files.

Wang and Wang [21] presented a malware recognition framework to ensure an accu-ray using the speculation capacity of support vector models (SVMs) by machine learning approach. The developed an automatic malware detection system trained the SVM clas-sifier based on behavioural patterns of each apk file. The SVMs associated with 60 existent malware families and performed a cross-validation scheme to resolve problems occurred in classification accuracy. For different sizing (N) of malware samples, the accuracy of the malware detection system reached up to 98.7% with N value is 100. The overall accuracy of the SVMs is more than 85% for unspecific multifaceted malware.

3.2 Anomaly or Behavioural Based Approaches

Haipeng Cai [29] implemented DroidCat, a novel dynamic app classification technique to characterizing system calls which are subject to system-call obfuscation. The 34,343 apps from various sources used for extracting the diverse set of dynamic features based on method calls and ICC Intents, system call and app resources. The potentially dangerous program behaviour was captured and analysed by DroidCat to resilient these types of attacks. The authors identified that method call distribution in libraries and code are imported rather than simply analysing the sensitive flow of the API. DroidCat achieved 97% F1-measure accuracy with higher robustness in dynamic classification. It showed 16% to 27% of higher performance as compared with the other bas line methods for detection and malware categorization. for our dynamic classification. We found that features capturing app execution structure such as the distribution of method calls over user code and libraries are much more important than typical security features such as sensitive flows.

Bhattacharya et al. [30] proposed a hybrid technique for permission feature based detection of malwares through AndroidManifest.xml file using machine learning clas-sifiers. Dataset contained total 734 applications which having 231 malwares and 504 benign files. The feature vector is generated and six feature reduction techniques are deployed to identify the most significant feature from the large feature set. Pearson Coefficient, Information Gain, Gain Ratio, Chi-Square, One R and Relief are the var-ious feature ranking methods implemented in the system. Weka, the data mining tool is used to perform the classification algorithms such as Bayesnet, Naive Bayes, SMO, Decision tree, Random Forest, Random Tree, J48 and MLP. The system showed that highest TPR rate as 98.01% while accuracy is run up to 87.99% and 0.9189 is the highest F1 score. The high false alarm and inaccuracy in the detection ratio due to the sparseness of the feature vector are the main two limitation of the study.

Mohaisen et al. [31] introduced an automatic behaviour based framework called AMAL, to address the malware classification problems. The proposed system consists of two subsystems named as AutoMal and MaLabel. AutoMal implemented to capture all the behaviour characteristics of malicious apks including file system usage, memory, network and registry and does that by running malware samples in virtualized domain. The other subsystem called MaLabel used these informations for feature representation and use them to construct classifiers trained using the manual evaluated training set. AutoMal is also capable to perform multiple grouping techniques. The recommend frameworks with two subsystems were evaluated on medium as well as large data sets contained 4000 and 15000 apks respectively. MaLabel exhibited 99.5% of precision and

Table 1. Study of signature based Android malware detection on selected articles

Method	Motive	Classification algorithm	Type of analysis	Type of detection	Dataset	Accuracy	Merits	Demerits
SOMM [17]	Service-oriented mobile malware detection system	DT, NB	Hybrid	Signature	Key Laboratory of Network Security, Fujian Normal University	97.3	High accuracy, High scaling	Not analysed behaviour of malwares due to high traffic
SIGPID [15]	Significant permission identification android malware detection	SVM	Dynamic	Signature	Google play store	94	Low cost, High accuracy	High time consumption
Opcode [16]	Opcode sequences	SVM, KNN	Hybrid	Signature	VXHeavens website	92.9	High unknown malware detection rate	Not analysed instance selection
SPM [18]	Sequential Pattern mining	J48, SVM, KNN, ANN	Hybrid	Signature	VXHeaven website	95.2	High accuracy, Low overhead	Feature selection is not analysed
SP-MDM [19]	Smartphone malware detection	K-means and Artificial immune system	Hybrid	Signature	Android malware database XVNA	89.8	Hybrid analysis used	Low accuracy, Not make classifier comparative study
SAAM [20]	Symbolic aggregate approximation for malwares	SVM & NB	Dynamic	Signature	Offensive computing and VX heavens library	95.9	High accuracy, Space complexity reduced	Not examine the multiple packing algorithms.
MobAMD [21]	Mobile android malware detection	SVM	Hybrid	Signature	Contagio Blogger and VirusTotal Websites	98.7	Good attribute selection, Low overhead	High complexity, Countermeasures not considered
DroidClassifier [22]	Droid malware detection	SVM	Dynamic	Signature	Windows API library	98	Fast feature selection	High complexity

(continued)

Table 1. (*continued*)

Method	Motive	Classification algorithm	Type of analysis	Type of detection	Dataset	Accuracy	Merits	Demerits
DroidNative [23]	Android malware detector with control flow patterns	Droid, CFGO-IL	Static	Signature	Several websites	93.57	High efficiency, Low time consumption	High cost, Low scalability
MKLDroid [24]	A multi-view context-ware approach to malware detection	Multiple Kernel Learning, SVM	Static	Signature	Google Play, AndroidDrawer, and FDroid	98.05	High efficiency Run time detection	High complexity, Not analysed feature selection
MDSyCall [25]	Malware detection using system call log	NB, RF	Static	Signature	Various Sources	98.5	High accuracy, Low time consumption	Small dataset, Only two classifiers
TinyDroid [26]	Malware detection and classification	RF, SVM, KNN, NB	Static	Signature	Drebin dataset	98.2	High accuracy, Low cost	Small dataset
DCSA [27]	Detection and classify malware	NB	Static	Signature	Google play and various android market	98	20 kinds of malware families were identified	API calls are not considered
ONAMD [28]	Online android malware detection	SVM, RF	Hybrid	Signature	Contagion mobile	87.83	Low accuracy	High time consumption

99.6% of recall for classification of malware family whereas unsupervised grouping resulted more than 98% precision and recall.

Altaher A [32] developed hybrid neuro-fuzzy classifier (EHNFC) for Android based malware grouping by employing the assent based components. The implemented EHNFC utilised the fuzzy rules for obfuscated malware detection and the detection accuracy was increased by learning new malware detection fuzzy rules using the structure of the obfuscated malware. To this end, employed various clustering techniques for adapting and fuzzy rules were updated to incorporate an adaptive procedure for upgrade the radii and centres of clustered permission-based features. The adjustments in the clustering methods improved the cluster convergence as well as assist to generate the better rules that are customised to the input data and showed increase in the classification accuracy. The system obtained 0.05 rates for both false negative and false positive. Compare with other neuro-fuzzy framework, the recommended system attained 90% classification accuracy.

Dali Z. et al. [33] suggested an automatic framework DeepFlow, to eliminate the problems in the malware classification using the various machine learning methods. The dataset consists of thousands of both benign and malware apk files from Google play store as well as virus share. The suggested system directly identified malware from the data flow in each apk files with taking the advantages of the deep learning-based approach. DeepFlow achieved high F1 score of 95.05% as compare with the conventional machine learning techniques.

Yuan Z. et al. [34] proposed online android malware characterisation model to couple the features from the static analysis to dynamic analysis features. The implemented online automatic framework called DroidDetector is investigated more than 20000 apk files used deep-learning algorithms for Android malware detection. Dataset comprised with 20000 benign apks and 1760 malware apks respectively from Goolge play store and Contagio Community and Genome Project. DroidDetector detection system utilised the Deep Belief Networks (DBN) and complicated neural networks for automatically classify the malware from benign apks. Various deep learning methods deployed to perform a deep level analysis in each android apps to determine the significant malware characteristics. Comparing all conventional machine learning algorithms, the DroidDetector obtained a high detection rate of 96.76%. In addition to this the framework is evaluated the 10 famous antivirus softwares to determine the necessity of android malware identification.

Abhishek Bhattacharya [35] introduced a static and dynamic android malware detection based on data mining techniques named as DMDAM. From different Android market, diverse categories of 170 apks samples were collected and which include 100 benign and 70 malware apps. The proposed a framework extracted the permission features from each manifest files of apk files and generated feature vectors. Different machine learning classifiers of a Data Mining Tool, Weka is used to classify android apk files. The system obtained that 96.70% as highest TPR rate and accuracy achieved up to 77.13% while highest F1score reached as 0.8583.

Nikolopoulos et al. [36] suggested a graph based model which detect the unknown malicious apk file and classify to known malware family by employing the relationships between the collections of system calls. The dataset prepared from different of commodity software types including various editors, media players, office suites etc.

Table 2. Study of anomaly or behavioral based Android malware detection on selected articles

Method	Motive	Classification algorithm	Type of analysis	Type of detection	Dataset	Accuracy	Merits	Demerits
DroidCat [29]	Malware Detection via App-Level Profiling	RF, SVM, NB, DT, KNN	Hybrid	Behavioural	Various Source	97	Low run time, High accuracy	Small dataset, Not explicitly considered all attacks
FRTMD [30]	Feature Ranking Techniques for Android Malware Detection	Bayes net, NB, SMO, DT, RF, Random Tree, J48 and MLP	Dynamic	Behavioural	Several websites	87.99	Identified most significant features, Low cost	High false alarm and sparseness of the feature vector leads to inaccuracy
AMAL [31]	Automated malware analysis	SVM, LR, KNN, Classification tree	Dynamic	Behavioural	Random sample from antivirus companies	98	High levels of precision, recall, and accuracy, Low cost	IP reputation High overhead
EHNFC [32]	Neuro–fuzzy classifier for malware detection	Evolving neuro fuzzy inference system	Static	Behavioural	Google play and Genome Project	90	High accuracy. Minimum false positive and false negative	Android apps Run-time overhead is not considered
DeepFlow [33]	Deep learning malware detection	NB, PART, LR, SVM and MLP	Hybrid	Behavioural	Google play, virus share	95.05	Directly capture the dataflow of malware	High time consumption

(continued)

Table 2. (*continued*)

Method	Motive	Classification algorithm	Type of analysis	Type of detection	Dataset	Accuracy	Merits	Demerits
DroidDetector [34]	Android Malware Characterization and Detection	Deep belief networks & complicated neural networks	Hybrid	Behavioural	Google play and Contagio Community and Genome Project.	96.76	Deployed online testing for Droiddetector	High cost, High overhead on API calls
DMDAM [35]	Android malware detection	Bayes net, NB, SMO, DT, J48, MLP, RF and Random Tree	Dynamic	Behavioural	Several Android applications	77.13	Reducing concepts for increasing feature selection	High complexity Run-time overhead
SyCM [36]	System-call malware	SaMe-NP	Dynamic	Behavioural	Variety of commodity software	95.9	High accuracy, High dependency analysis for system calls	Time consumption increased
DFAMD [37]	Data flow android malware detection	KNN, LR, NB	Static	Behavioural	VXHeavens website and Google play	97.66	High efficiency, Low overhead, Low time	High complexity, High dependency
RanDroid [38]	Android malware detection using random machine learning classifiers	Long Short-Term Memory (LSTM)	Hybrid	Behavioural	Benign AndroZoo and Malware from AMD	98.98	High Accuracy, First used chronological dataset	High time consumption

(*continued*)

Table 2. (continued)

Method	Motive	Classification algorithm	Type of analysis	Type of detection	Dataset	Accuracy	Merits	Demerits
DNNMD [39]	Deep Neural Networks for Android Malware Detection	CNN and LSTM	Static	Behavioural	Drebin Dataset, FdroidGooglePlay and AndroZoo	95.3	Large Dataset	No dynamic implementation
DRAI [40]	Detecting Data Residue in Android Images	CFG	Static	Behavioural	Various sources	86.53	Identified new data residue instances	Low accuracy
EnDroid [41]	Malware detection with ensemble learning	SVM, NB, KNN, DT, RF, Xgboost,	Dynamic	Behavioural	Google Plays store and Derbin dataset	97.17	High accuracy	Small dataset
DBAA [42]	Dynamic behaviour of android Apps	DT, RF, KNN, ANN, SVM	Dynamic	Behavioural	Google Play Store	97.16	Identified large set of malicious system calls	Small apk samples set

and contained 2667 apk files. With the help of the System-call Dependency Graphs (or, for short, ScD-graphs) is obtained by traces captured through dynamic taint analysis. The Authors have implemented strong modifications in detection as well as classification methods on a weighted directed graph, namely Group Relation Graph, or Gr-graph for short, outcome from ScD-graph after grouping disjoint subsets of its vertices. The Δ-similarity metric proposed for detection process whereas SaMe-similarity and NP-similarity metrics consisting the SaMe-NP similarity presented for classification. The proposed system exhibited 95.9% classification accuracy.

Wu S. et al. [37] implemented a novel automatic system to detect malicious behavior in the apk files based on the data flow application program interfaces (APIs). The dataset contained more than two thousands apks from the Google play store and various third-party stores. Dataflow-related API features were extracted and the list is further optimised to find the most significant features by utilizing the various machine learning techniques. The k-nearest neighbour implemented as classification model. The proposed framework exhibited 97.66% accuracy in detecting unknown Android malware. More than that, Static dataflow analysis resulted more than 85% of sensitive data transmission paths can be identified with the assist of the refined API subset.

J. D. Koli [38] presented an integrated machine learning approach for android malware detection. The experimental dataset included with 10010 benign apps from Andro-Zoo and 10683 malwares from AMD. In addition to this, the author evaluated the accuracy of malware and benign apksby sent some of the samples to the popular 4 anti-virus scanners such as Kingsoft Antivirus, McAfee, Norton, 360 Security Guard. The author flagged the apps as malware when it is detected by one or more of these scanners. The API informations were obtained by the control flow graph (CFG) of each apk file and three different datasets were built by utilizing the API informations such as Boolean, frequency and chronological data sets. The three detection systems were deployed from these three data sets to identify malware characteristic based on API calls, API frequency, and API sequence. The ensemble detection model achieved 98.98% detection accuracy. The API Usage Detection Model detects 95% of the malware samples with a false-positive rate of 6.2%. The API Frequency Detection Model identified 97% of the malware samples with a false-positive rate of 9.1%. The 2.9% false positive rate was exhibited by the API Sequence Detection Model with detection rate 99%. The proposed statistical detection system was the first to construct chronological datasets of the Android application and constructed the detection model based on the Long Short-Term Memory (LSTM) algorithm.

AbhilashHota and Paul Irolla [39] implemented deep neural network based android malware detection system. The proposed framework evaluated for two different data sets. The first contained 3500 malware from the Drebin Dataset and 2700 benign from Fdroid. The second dataset contained 7,412,461 apk samples taken from Google play store as well as the AndroZoo. The four different models were generated such as Convolutional neural networks (CNN) with three 2D convolutional layers model, CNN with 10000 length document vector model, MalConv architecture based model and finally LSTM model. Each models where evaluated with these two different datasets and the LSTM model with dataset 2 have achieved 95.3% detection rate.

Y. Zhou et al. [40] suggested a statistical model an ANdroidREsidue Detector (ANRED) to analyse the bytecode and automatically evaluate the risk for each determined data reside instance. ANRED dataset consists of 606 android images collected from different sources and implemented in WALA. The system took the input as the entire android image and extracted the features as apps bytecode. The framework implemented with two operations such as Saving and Deleting operations as well as the result generated two different graph as Saving graph and Deleting graph. All the data saved inside the framework were expressed in saving graph whereas the deleting graph depicted the removed data when app uninstallation. From the traditional systems, the accuracy and efficiency are increased in ANRED and identified 5 new residue vulnerabilities.

3.3 Topic Modeling Approaches

A. Gorla [43] proposed a system for checking app behaviour against app descriptions named as CHABADA. The system compared the implemented app behavior with the app description using 22521 free android apps from Google play store. The Natural Language Processing technique is used for filtering and stemming, for that Google's Compact Language Detector is used. The output of NLP [12] pre-processing (i.e., the English text without stop words, and after stemming) fed into the Mallet framework. The LDA [11] used on the app description to generate topic model. Apps were clustered with K means algorithm and 32 clusters were formed, that an app would belongs to 4 topics. The unsupervised One-Class SVM anomaly classification method is performed on the system. CHABADA identified outliers with respect to API usage and used set of sensitive APIs derived from STOWAWAY. CHABADA flagged 56% of known malware as such, without requiring any training on malware patterns. The Static analysis was conducted down on the Dalvikbyte code and not on native code.

Chengpeng Zhang [44] conducted study on CHABADA and designed Re-checking App Behavior against App Description. Around 400,000 free android apps were downloaded from Google play store and analysed the impact of third-party libraries (TPLs) separate TPLs from app custom code and determine whether the sensitive behaviors are introduced by custom code. The authors crawled the metadata of these apps, including the app names, app categories, app ratings, the number of installs, etc. along with the apk files of these apps. The system takes the advantage of Mallet for building a list to filter out stop-words. Then Snowball used to turn the words into stem form. A list of permission-related APIs was collected from PScout [41], which contains 680 sensitive APIs. At last, there are only 428 APIs left to apply Genetic Algorithm (GA) combined with K-means ++ to determine the best number of clusters and 30 topic clusters identified. As per the outlier detection using Isolation Forest algorithm with and without TPLs is resulted respectively as 46.5% and 49.9% whereas the detection results of VirusTotal in false positive and false negative apps are 24.7% and 49.65% respectively.

R. Pandita [45] proposed a system WHYPER for automating the risk assessment of mobile applications with a dataset contained top 500 free applications in each category of the Google Play Store (16,001 total unique applications). The framework consists of five components such as a pre-processor, an NLP Parser, an intermediate representation generator, a semantic engine (SE), and an analyser. The pre-processor accepts application descriptions and pre-processes the sentences in the descriptions, such as annotating sentence boundaries and reducing lexical tokens. The intermediate representation generator accepts the pre-processed sentences and parses them using an NLP parser. The parsed sentences are then transformed into the first-order-logic (FOL) representation. SE accepts the FOL representation of a sentence and annotates the sentence based on the semantic graphs of permissions. WHYPER effectively identifies permission sentences with the average precision, recall, F-score, and accuracy of 80.1%, 78.6%, 79.3%, and 97.3% respectively. WHYPER performs better than keyword-based search with an average increase in precision of 40% with a relatively small decrease in average recall (1.2%). The semantic information, associated APIs and automation are limited in the proposed static model.

Z. Qu [46] presented a system AutoCog that measures the description-to-permissions fidelity in Android, i.e., whether the permissions requested by Android applications match or can be inferred from the applications' descriptions. The dataset contained the declared permissions and descriptions of 37,845 Android applications from Google Play. The use of a novel learning-based algorithm and advanced NLP techniques allows us to mine relationships between textual patterns and permissions. AutoCog matches human in inferring 11 permissions with the average precision, recall, F-score, and accuracy as 92.6%, 92.0%, 92.3%, and 93.2% respectively. Permission is used as an only feature where manual reading is subjective and the results may be biased. However, given that the authors have a technical background, they may be able to discover many implicit relationships that average users ignore, thus putting up greater challenges for AutoCog.

Eric Medvet [47] explored the usage of topic modeling methods in android malware static analysis. Dataset contains 900 Android malware applications which obtained from Drebin Dataset with 49 malware families. LDA is applied to Android applications rather than to texts. In particular, considered an application as a sequence of opcodes, hence topics are distributions of opcodes rather the distributions of words. Then clustered applications based on their coordinates in the topics space, that is, a low dimension space where each coordinate represents a topic. The five different clustering techniques were applied on the model. The cumulative percent of variance explained is 57:9%, 21:2%, and 21:4% respectively for the features, opcode frequencies, and topics spaces. Higher level features deriving from the topic space may help in improving the effectiveness of fully-automatic detection techniques based on opcodes.

Mayank Garg [48] classified the apps effectively and identified outlier apps with the help of app behavior analysis. Crawler is used to extract app content such as App title and App description from the 600 apps of 10 categories from Google play store with description word length is 404 and NLP is applied for text pre-processing. Then first performed the Non negative matrix factorization topic modeling technique to generate feature vector list on the basis of App description and used probabilistic approach Latent Dirichlet Allocation (LDA) which helps in upgrading, associating feature vector list and further assign probability to features available in feature vector list. The clusters have been formed according to features based classification using K nearest neighbour algorithm which will place all the classified Apps in suitable clusters based on features similarity measure. If features shown to users in description are not similar to accessed or mentioned in manifest file it will treat such apps as outlier app or malevolent App. According to the classification results, the Music cluster contains 12.1% apps, from

Table 3. Study of topic modeling based Android malware detection on selected articles

Method	Motive	Classification algorithm	Topic modeling method	Type of analysis	Type of detection	Dataset	Result	Merits	Demerits
CHABADA [43]	Checking app behaviour against app descriptions	K-means, SVM	LDA	Static	Signature & Behavioural	Google play store	54	Identified outlier apps with APIs	Native code not analysed
ReCHABADA [44]	Re-checking app behaviour against app description	K-means++	LDA	Static	Behavioural	Google play store	60.19	Impact of third-party libraries (TPLs) considered	Complexity is high
WHYPER [45]	Automating Risk Assessment apks	Statistical Classifier	LSA	Hybrid	Behavioural	Google Play Store	97.3	High Accuracy	The semantic information, associated APIs and automation are limited
AutoCog [46]	Description to permissions fidelity in Android	–	LSA	Hybrid	Signature	Google Play Store	93.2	High Accuracy, Extracted implicit relationships	Difficult in identification of implicit relationships.
TMAW [47]	Topic modeling methods in android malware	K-Means	LDA	Static	Signature	Drebin Dataset, Google Play Store	57.9 cumulative percent of variance	Malware characteristics and similarities identified	Not automatic detection techniques

(continued)

Table 3. (*continued*)

Method	Motive	Classification algorithm	Topic modeling method	Type of analysis	Type of detection	Dataset	Result	Merits	Demerits
IOPB [48]	Identified outlier apps with permission behavior	K-Nearest Neighbour, K mean	NMF (Nonnegative matrix factorization), LDA	Static	Behavioural	Google play store	95	Identified 5% of outlier apks	Extracted Feature vector not enough to identify android behaviour
ActSSB [49]	Active semi-supervised approach for checking app behavior against its description	Semi-Supervised Labeling (ECASSL) algorithm, SVM	LDA-GA	Static	Behavioural	Various Sources	96.02	High Accuracy	External validity not considered
AppLibRec [50]	Recommend third party libraries for mobile apps	Statistical Classifier	LDA	Hybrid	Behavioural	Randomly from GitHub	43.46 precision	Third party libraries are analysed	Not contain the sufficient co-occurrence of third party libraries.
TDFS [51]	Topic specific dataflow signatures	–	LDA, LDA-GD	Static	Signature	Google Play and Best Apps Market	Sensitive data flow analyzed	Sensitive data flow signatures is used	Small dataset
ReLDA [52]	Topics of each mobile app	–	LDA, CombineLDA	Static	Signature	Google Play store	56 F Measure	Users Recommendations were analysed	Android apk file is not even considered

that 5% app in the cluster are detected as outlier apps. The study limited in the static analysis whereas proposed system is not robust enough to reflect android behaviour. Each permission governs several APIs using permission alone would give too few features. Therefore instead of just using manifest file, the sensitive API can be used to get more fine grained permission.

Siqi Ma [49] implemented an active semi-supervised approach for checking app behavior against its description. The dataset contained 22,555 apps with 172 malicious and 22,383 benign android apps. The stop-word removal and stemming are performed with the help of NLP techniques. The LDA-GA (Latent Dirichlet Allocation-Genetic Algorithm) algorithm combines LDA algorithm with genetic algorithm (GA) applied to generated topic models. App feature are extracted with the help of Apktool and collected 304 sensitive API methods. The feature vector is analysed with the Ensured Collaborative Active and Semi-Supervised Labeling (ECASSL) algorithm, which combines semi-supervised learning (SSL) and active learning (AL) and is built on top of SVM. When using 10% of the entire data as training data, the system achieved as a precision of 100%, recall of 91.23%, and F-measure of 95.41%.

Huan Yu [50] proposed an automated hybrid approach AppLibRec that combines topic model and collaborative filtering to recommend third party libraries for mobile apps. The dataset contains randomly downloaded 3,117 mobile applications from GitHub. The proposed system performed two kinds of analysis such as based on textual description and library. AppLibRec approach extracted topics from the textual description of app and given new app, as well as recommends libraries based on the libraries used by the apps which has similar topic distributions. The system outperformed the state-of-the-art approach by a substantial margin. Experiments results show that the precision and recall of LibRec by 38% and 35%, respectively.

Xinli Yang [51] characterized malicious android apps by mining topic-specific dataflow signatures. Dataset contains 3691 benign and 1612 malicious apps and crawled descriptions of apps from Google Play Store and Best Apps Market for benign and malicious apps respectively. NLTK used for extract the app description features with the representative terms and used their term frequency as features. A topic model is built with the extracted features using adaptive LDA with Genetic Algorithm (GA). GA is used to determine the optimal number of topics and each topic-specific signature will include fewer, specific, data flow patterns each data-flow signature contains more discriminative information to identify malicious apps in a specific topic. Each data flow signature characterizes more fine-grained behavior of malicious apps in this topic by highlighting the specific data-flow patterns that they are prone to exhibit.

Tianho Pan [52] presented a CombineLDA to analyse different topics of each mobile app and calculate the similarity and user comments with high similarity apps. Top 5 Mobile Phone applications are taken for the experiment. Android recommendation result shows that precision and recall as 0.41 and 0.15 respectively. LDA with user comments is resulted as 0.36 as precision and 0.13 as recall. Finally combineLDA precision and recall as 0.47 and 0.19 respectively. The analysis conducted only on android recommendation and User comments where android apk file is not even considered.

4 Evaluation of Selected Articles

The investigation is conducted on the different malware detection approaches namely signature based, anomaly or behavioural based and topic modelling based. The diverse frameworks were evaluated across their motives, classification algorithms used, analysis types, detection types, dataset source, accuracy and finally the merits and demerits of the implemented system (Refer Table 1, 2 and 3). The table informations are again evaluated by the pictorial representations. The Fig. 5 depicts the accuracy achieved by the various systems in the selected study based on the detection approaches. In signature based approach, MDSyCall [25] showed highest accuracy as 98.5% with Naive Bayes and Random Forest classifiers. But the disadvantage of this static system is the small sample set. ONAMD [28] system got the lowest accuracy as 87.83% with support vector machine and random forest classifiers. This hybrid method exhibited low accuracy may be the limitations of online validation approache.

RanDroid [38] system obtained 98.98% high detection rate in the case of behavioural based systems. But the time consumption is a demerit for this hybrid framework. In the same time, it contained a large collection of apk files and it made use of the advantages of the LSTM technique. The authors proposed a dynamic system called DMDAM [35] shows very low accuracy rate as 77.13%. The system utilising different classifiers to analyse the best detection rate but also it failed to improve the run time overheads in anomaly based analysis. In the case of topic modelling based approaches the WHYPER [45] framework exhibits a high accuracy as 97.3% and the sematic informations were associated with the APIs to classify the malware in the behaviour based hybrid system. The topic modelling based studies are concentrated on the test feature analysis from the user reviews, recommendations and comments etc. There extracted feature were further classified to analyses the malware apk files. The term "topic" is somewhat ambigious, and topic models will not produce highly nuanced classification of texts. This is a major disadvantage in the topic modeling technique.

Similarly, Fig. 6 depicts that the 38.4% of static and hybrid approaches were applied on the selected signature based articles whereas the dynamic analysis got only 23%. This is because of the zero day attacks are failed on the signature based method. In the behavioural based approach, the execution of the android application is closely watched with the help of the special sandbox approached. Hence the dynamic based analysis is always preferred in the behavioural system to investigate the delvik code and native code. Figure 6 is also resulting that 42.8% of dynamic analysis in implemented in behavioural models. The topic based systems repeatedly utilized both static as well as the dynamic methods for malware analysis. This shows 70% of the studied papers were contributing the hybrid approach.

In addition to this, various classifiers were used in the selected study papers. The Fig. 7 explains the percentages of each classifiers used in all the selected articles. The Support Vector Machine (SVM) is the most widely used grouping techniques because it is a supervised machine learning algorithm which can be used for both classification and regression applications. The second place 12% occupied by the Naive Bayes (NB) classifier which works based on Bayes' Theorem with an assumption of independence among predictors. In simple terms, a Naive Bayes classifier assumes that the presence of a particular feature in a class is unrelated to the presence of any other feature. The

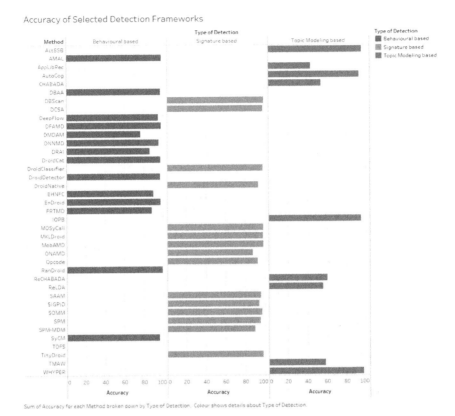

Fig. 5. Accuracy of the selected frameworks based on the detection methods

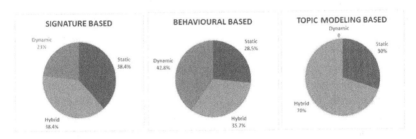

Fig. 6. Percentage of different analysis types used with malware detection approaches

K- Nearest Neighbours (KNN) got the next position with 11%. The KNN algorithm is supervised; it takes a bunch of labelled points and uses them to learn how to label other points. RandomForest (RF) and Decision Tree (DT) are shared 10% and 7% respectively. Decision Tree builds classification or regression models in the form of a tree structure. It breaks down a data set into smaller and smaller subsets while at the same time an associated decision tree is incrementally developed. Random decision forests correct for decision trees' habit of over fitting to their training set. The other grouping methods come below 5% for rest of the article selected for the evaluation.

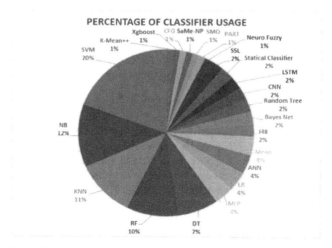

Fig. 7. Percentage of various classifiers usage in the selected articles

5   Conclusion

This paper analysed the various android malware detection approaches and analysis types. The selected articles are inspected to determine the utilisation of each malware detection methods. Signature based method is always failed to address the zero-day attacks. Hence the behavioural based approached are preferred always. Topic modeling is an emerging technique to classify the android malware based on their description, user reviews and commands etc. The text features are extracted and evaluated to conduct the grouping operations. Topic modelling approached are combined with the signature or anomaly based method to achieve a good results. In addition to this, static analysis is considering patters or signature of the apk sample for investigations which not focuses to code level analysis. Dynamic solutions produce the best results in the android malware detection especially in the code obfuscation attacks. Most of the proposed frameworks are implemented with hybrid approaches by make use of the static and dynamic merits. Machine learning techniques were deployed for grouping and SVM classifier showed high detection rate in android malware classification.

References

1. https://www.statista.com/statistics/330695/number-of-smartphone-users-worldwide. Accessed June 2019
2. http://gs.statcounter.com/os-market-share/mobile/worldwide. Accessed May 2019

3. https://www.mcafee.com/enterprise/en-us/assets/reports/rp-mobile-threat-report-2019.pdf. Accessed April 2019
4. https://www.kaspersky.co.in/resource-center/threats/mobile. Accessed July 2019
5. https://securelist.com/it-threat-evolution-q1-2019-statistics/90916/. Accessed May 2019
6. https://www.appbrain.com/stats/number-of-android-apps. Accessed July 2019
7. Mobile Banking Trojans on Android OS. https://www.computerworld.com/article/2475964/98–of-mobile-malware-targets-android-platform.html. Accessed 27 Nov 2018
8. Peng, S., Yu, S., Yang, A.: Smartphone malware and its propagation modeling: a survey. IEEE Commun. Surv. Tutor. **16**(2), 925–941 (2014). https://doi.org/10.1109/SURV.2013.070813.00214
9. Sabillon, R., Cavaller, V., Cano, J., Serra-Ruiz, J.: Cybercriminals, cyberattacks and cyber-crime. In: 2016 IEEE International Conference on Cybercrime and Computer Forensic (ICCCF), Vancouver, BC, pp. 1–9 (2016). https://doi.org/10.1109/icccf.2016.7740434
10. Qu, Z., Alam, S., Chen, Y., Zhou, X., Hong, W., Riley, R.: DyDroid: measuring dynamic code loading and its security implications in android applications. In: 2017 47th Annual IEEE/IFIP International Conference on Dependable Systems and Networks (DSN), Denver, CO, pp. 415–426 (2017). https://doi.org/10.1109/dsn.2017.14
11. Blei, D.M., Ng, A.Y., Jordan, M.I.: Latent dirichlet allocation. J. Mach. Learn. Res. **3**, 993–1022 (2003)
12. Gelbukh, A.: Natural language processing. In: Fifth International Conference on Hybrid Intelligent Systems (HIS 2005), Rio de Janeiro, Brazil, pp. 1–pp (2005). https://doi.org/10.1109/ichis.2005.79
13. Allix, K., Bissyandé, T.F., Jérome, Q., Klein, J., State, R., Le Traon, Y.: Empirical assessment of machine learning-based malware detectors for Android. Empirical Softw. Eng. **21**(1), 183–211 (2014). https://doi.org/10.1007/s10664-014-9352-6
14. Winsniewski, R.: Android–Apktool: a tool for reverse engineering Android APK files. Technical report (2012)
15. Li, J., Sun, L., Yan, Q., Li, Z., Srisa-an, W., Ye, H.: Significant permission identification for machine-learning-based Android malware detection. IEEE Trans. Ind. Inform. **14**(7), 3216–3225 (2018). https://doi.org/10.1109/TII.2017.2789219
16. Santos, I., Brezo, F., Ugarte-Pedrero, X.: Opcode sequences as representation of executables for data mining-based unknown malware detection. Inf. Sci. **231**, 64–82 (2013). https://doi.org/10.1016/j.ins.2011.08.020
17. Cui, B., Jin, H., Carullo, G., Liu, Z.: Service-oriented mobile malware detection system based on mining strategies. Pervasive Mob. Comput. **24**, 101–116 (2015). https://doi.org/10.1016/j.pmcj.2015.06.006
18. Fan, Y., Ye, Y., Chen, L.: Malicious sequential pattern mining for automatic malware detection. Expert Syst. Appl. **52**, 16–25 (2016). https://doi.org/10.1016/j.eswa.2016.01.002
19. Wu, B., Lu, T., Zheng, K., Zhang, D., Lin, X.: Smartphone malware detection model based on artificial immune system. China Commun. **11**, 86–92 (2014). https://doi.org/10.1109/CC.2014.7022530
20. Bat-Erdene, M., Park, H., Li, H., Lee, H., Choi, M.-S.: Entropy analysis to classify unknown packing algorithms for malware detection. Int. J. Inf. Secur. **16**(3), 227–248 (2016). https://doi.org/10.1007/s10207-016-0330-4
21. Wang, P., Wang, Y.-S.: Malware behavioural detection and vaccine development by using a support vector model classifier. J. Comput. Syst. Sci. **81**, 1012–1026 (2015). https://doi.org/10.1016/j.jcss.2014.12.014
22. Li, Z., Sun, L., Yan, Q., Srisa-an, W., Chen, Z.: DroidClassifier: efficient adaptive mining of application-layer header for classifying Android malware. In: Deng, R., Weng, J., Ren, K., Yegneswaran, V. (eds.) SecureComm 2016. LNICST, vol. 198, pp. 597–616. Springer, Cham (2017). https://doi.org/10.1007/978-3-319-59608-2_33

23. Alam, S., Qu, Z., Riley, R., Chen, Y., Rastogi, V.: DroidNative: automating and optimizing detection of Android native code malware variants. Comput. Secur. **65**, 230–246 (2017). https://doi.org/10.1016/j.cose.2016.11.011

24. Narayanan, A., Chandramohan, M., Chen, L., Liu, Y.: A multi-view context-aware approach to Android malware detection and malicious code localization. Empirical Softw. Eng. **23**(3), 1222–1274 (2017). https://doi.org/10.1007/s10664-017-9539-8

25. Chaba, S., Kumar, R., Pant, R., Dave, M.: Malware detection approach for android systems using system call logs. Cryptography and Security. arXiv:1709.08805

26. Chen, T., Mao, Q., Yang, Y., Lv, M., Zhu, J.: TinyDroid: a lightweight and efficient model for Android malware detection and classification. Mob. Inf. Syst. **2018**, 9 (2018). https://doi.org/10.1155/2018/4157156. Article ID 4157156

27. Kang, H., Jang, J., Mohaisen, A., Kim, H.K.: Detecting and classifying Android malware using static analysis along with creator information. Int. J. Distrib. Sens. Netw. (2015). https://doi.org/10.1155/2015/479174

28. Riasat, R., Sakeena, M.: Onamd: an online Android malware detection approach. In: International Conference on Machine Learning and Cybernetics (ICMLC), July 2018. https://doi.org/10.1109/icmlc.2018.8526997

29. Cai, H., Meng, N., Ryder, B., Yao, D.: DroidCat: effective Android malware detection and categorization via app-level profiling. IEEE Trans. Inf. Forensics Secur. **14**(6), 1455–1470 (2018). https://doi.org/10.1109/TIFS.2018.2879302

30. Bhattacharya, A., Goswami, R.T.: Comparative analysis of different feature ranking techniques in data mining-based Android malware detection. In: Satapathy, S.C., Bhateja, V., Udgata, S.K., Pattnaik, P.K. (eds.) Proceedings of the 5th International Conference on Frontiers in Intelligent Computing: Theory and Applications. AISC, vol. 515, pp. 39–49. Springer, Singapore (2017). https://doi.org/10.1007/978-981-10-3153-3_5

31. Mohaisen, A., Alrawi, O., Mohaisen, M.: AMAL: high-fidelity, behavior-based automated malware analysis and classification. Comput. Secur. **52**, 251–266 (2015). https://doi.org/10.1016/j.cose.2015.04.001

32. Altaher, A.: An improved Android malware detection scheme based on an evolving hybrid neuro-fuzzy classifier (EHNFC) and permission-based features. Neural Comput. Appl. **28**(12), 4147–4157 (2016). https://doi.org/10.1007/s00521-016-2708-7

33. Dali, Z., Hao, J., Ying, Y., Wu, D., Weiyi, C.: DeepFlow: deep learning-based malware detection by mining Android application for abnormal usage of sensitive data. In: 2017 IEEE Symposium on Computers and Communications (ISCC), pp 438–443 (2017)

34. Yuan, Z., Lu, Y., Xue, Y.: Droiddetector: Android malware characterization and detection using deep learning. Tsinghua Sci. Technol. **21**, 114–123 (2016). https://doi.org/10.1109/TST.2016.7399288

35. Bhattacharya, A., Goswami, R.T.: DMDAM: data mining based detection of Android malware. In: Mandal, J., Satapathy, S., Sanyal, M., Bhateja, V. (eds.) Proceedings of the First International Conference on Intelligent Computing and Communication. AISC, vol. 458, pp. 187–194. Springer, Singapore (2017). https://doi.org/10.1007/978-981-10-2035-3_20

36. Nikolopoulos, S.D., Polenakis, I.: A graph-based model for malware detection and classification using system-call groups. J. Comput. Virol. Hacking Tech. **13**(1), 29–46 (2016). https://doi.org/10.1007/s11416-016-0267-1

37. Wu, S., Wang, P., Li, X., Zhang, Y.: Effective detection of Android malware based on the usage of data flow APIs and machine learning. Inf. Softw. Technol. **75**, 17–25 (2016). https://doi.org/10.1016/j.infsof.2016.03.004

38. Koli, J.D.: RanDroid: Android malware detection using random machine learning classifiers. In: IEEE Technologies for Smart-City Energy Security and Power (ICSESP), Bhubaneswar, pp. 1–6 (2018). https://doi.org/10.1109/icsesp.2018.8376705

39. Hota, A., Irolla, P.: Deep neural networks for Android malware detection
40. Zhou, Y., Wang, Z., Zhou, W., Jiang, X.: Hey you get off of my market: detecting malicious apps in official and alternative Android markets. In: Proceedings of the Annual Network and Distributed System Security Symposium, vol. 25, no. 4, pp. 50–52 (2012)
41. Feng, P., Ma, J., Sun, C., Xu, X., Ma, Y.: A novel dynamic Android malware detection system with ensemble learning. IEEE Access **6**, 30996–31011 (2018). https://doi.org/10.1109/ACC ESS.2018.2844349
42. Singh, L., Hofmann, M.: Dynamic behavior analysis of Android applications for malware detection. In: 2017 International Conference on Intelligent Communication and Computational Techniques (ICCT), Jaipur, pp. 1–7 (2017). https://doi.org/10.1109/intelcct.2017.832 4010
43. Gorla, A., Tavecchia, I., Gross, F., Zeller, A.: Checking app behavior against app descriptions. In: ICSE 2014 Proceedings of the 36th International Conference on Software Engineering, Hyderabad, India, 31 May–07 June 2014, pp. 1025–1035. ACM, New York (2014). https:// doi.org/10.1145/2568225.2568276
44. Zhang, C., Wang, H., Wang, R., Guo, Y., Xu, G.: Re-checking app behavior against app description in the context of third-party libraries. In: SEKE 2018 (2018). https://doi.org/10. 18293/seke2018-180
45. Pandita, R., Xiao, X., Yang, W., Enck, W., Xie, T.: WHYPER: towards automating risk assessment of mobile applications. In: USENIX Security 2013, pp. 527–542 (2013)
46. Qu, Z., Rastogi, V., Zhang, X., Chen, Y., Zhu, T., Chen, Z.: AutoCog: measuring the description-to-permission fidelity in Android applications. In: ICCS 2014, pp. 1354–1365 (2014)
47. Medvet, E., Mercaldo, F.: Exploring the usage of topic modeling for Android malware static analysis. In: 2016 11th International Conference on Availability, Reliability and Security (ARES), Salzburg, pp. 609–617 (2016). https://doi.org/10.1109/ares.2016.10
48. Garg, M., Monga, A., Bhatt, P., Arora, A.: Android app behaviour classification using topic modeling techniques and outlier detection using app permissions. In: 2016 Fourth International Conference on Parallel, Distributed and Grid Computing (PDGC), Waknaghat, pp. 500–506 (2016). https://doi.org/10.1109/pdgc.2016.7913246
49. Ma, S., Wang, S., Lo, D., Deng, R.H., Sun, C.: Active semi-supervised approach for checking app behavior against its description. In: 2015 IEEE 39th Annual Computer Software and Applications Conference, Taichung, pp. 179–184 (2015). https://doi.org/10.1109/COM PSAC.2015.93
50. Yu, H., Xia, X., Zhao, X., Qiu, W.: Combining collaborative filtering and topic modeling for more accurate Android mobile app library recommendation. In: Internetware 2017 Proceedings of the 9th Asia-Pacific Symposium on Internetware, Shanghai, China, 23 September 2017. ACM, New York (2017). Article no. 17. https://doi.org/10.1145/3131704.3131721
51. Yang, X., Lo, D., Li, L., Xia, X., Bissyandé, T.F., Klein, J.: Characterizing malicious Android apps by mining topic-specific data flow signatures. Inf. Softw. Technol. **90**, 27–39 (2017). https://doi.org/10.1016/j.infsof.2017.04.007
52. Pan, T., Zhang, W., Wang, Z., Xu, L.: Recommendations based on LDA topic model in Android applications. In: 2016 IEEE International Conference on Software Quality, Reliability and Security Companion (QRS-C), Vienna, pp. 151–158 (2016). https://doi.org/10.1109/qrs-c. 2016.24

DCNN-IDS: Deep Convolutional Neural Network Based Intrusion Detection System

S. Sriram[1(✉)], A. Shashank[1], R. Vinayakumar[1,2], and K. P. Soman[1]

[1] Center for Computational Engineering and Networking,
Amrita School of Engineering, Amrita Vishwa Vidyapeetham, Coimbatore, India
sri27395ram@gmail.com, vinayakumarr77@gmail.com
[2] Division of Biomedical Informatics, Cincinnati Children's Hospital Medical Centre,
Cincinnati, OH, USA
Vinayakumar.Ravi@cchmc.org

Abstract. In the present era, cyberspace is growing tremendously and the intrusion detection system (IDS) plays a key role in it to ensure information security. The IDS, which works in network and host level, should be capable of identifying various malicious attacks. The job of network-based IDS is to differentiate between normal and malicious traffic data and raise an alert in case of an attack. Apart from the traditional signature and anomaly-based approaches, many researchers have employed various deep learning (DL) techniques for detecting intrusion as DL models are capable of extracting salient features automatically from the input data. The application of deep convolutional neural network (DCNN), which is utilized quite often for solving research problems in image processing and vision fields, is not explored much for IDS. In this paper, a DCNN architecture for IDS which is trained on KDDCUP 99 data set is proposed. This work also shows that the DCNN-IDS model performs superior when compared with other existing works.

Keywords: Intrusion detection · Deep learning · Convolutional neural network · Cyber security

1 Introduction

Information Technology (IT) systems play a key role in handling several sensitive user data that are prone to several external and internal intruder attacks [1]. Every day, the attackers are coming up with new sophisticated attacks and the attacks against IT systems are growing as the internet grows. As a result, a novel, reliable and flexible IDS is necessary to handle the security threats like malware attacks which could compromise a network of systems that can be used by the attackers to perform various attacks using command and control servers. Though there are various other security systems like firewall, IDS plays a major role in defending the network from all kinds of cyberattacks. IDS is divided into

S. Balusamy et al. (Eds.): ICC3 2019, CCIS 1213, pp. 85–92, 2020.
https://doi.org/10.1007/978-981-15-9700-8_7

two categories. The first one is network IDS (NIDS) which monitors the network traffic and raises alerts when it detects any kind of attack. The second one is host-based IDS (HIDS) which detects both internal and external intrusion and misuse by monitoring the system in which it is installed. It constantly records the user activities and alerts the designated authority in case of an attack. Both IDS are represented in Fig. 1.

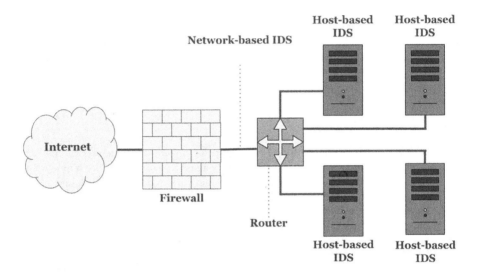

Fig. 1. Model of IDS

The job of NIDS is to monitor the network traffic and to identify whether the network traffic records as either malicious or normal (benign). Several machine learning (ML) and deep learning (DL) classifiers are widely employed for the detection of intrusion as it is a classification problem. DL models like autoencoders (AE), recurrent structures, deep neural network (DNN), etc. are used for IDS by many researchers. The convolutional neural network (CNN) model is quite often utilized for solving research problems in fields like computer vision, image processing, etc. due to its capability to extract location invariant features automatically. The application of CNN for IDS is not explored much. Therefore, in this paper, deep CNN (DCNN) is trained on the most popular benchmark data set called KDDCup 99 which has more than 8,00,000 data points. It is also shown that the DCNN-IDS gives superior outcomes when compared to previous works. Further, this paper is arranged as follows. Sections 2 and 3 includes the related works and data set description. Sections 4 and 5 describes the statistical measures and the proposed model respectively. Sections 6 and 7 covers the results and conclusion.

2   Related Works

Several ML based approaches are proposed for IDS. [2] analyses several ML based approaches for intrusion detection for identifying various issues. Issues related to the detection of low-frequency attacks are discussed with possible solutions to improve the performance further. The disadvantage of ML based approach is that ML models operate on manual features extracted by the domain expert. Since DL models can extract relevant features automatically without human intervention, many researchers propose various DL based solution for IDS. Self-Taught learning based NIDS is proposed in [3], where a sparse autoencoder and softmax regression is used. The proposed model is trained on the NSLKDD data set and it achieves an accuracy around 79.10% for 5-class classification which is very close to the performance of existing models. Apart from this, 23-class and 2-class classification also achieved good performance. A recent study [4] claims that the deep networks perform better than shallow networks for IDS as the deep network is capable of learning salient features by mapping the input through various layers. In [5], the performance of RNN based NIDS is studied. The model is trained on the NSL-KDD data set and both multi-class and binary classification are performed. The performance of RNN based IDS is far superior in both classification when compared to other traditional approaches and the author claims that RNN based IDS has strong modeling capabilities for IDS. Similarly in [6] and [7], various recurrent structures are proposed for IDS.

In [8], a new stacked non-symmetric deep autoencoder (NDAE) based NIDS is proposed. The model is trained on both KDDCUP and NSLKDD benchmark data sets and its performance is compared with DBN based model. It can be observed from the experimental analysis that the NDAE based approach improves the accuracy up to 5% with 98.8% training time reduction when compared to DBN based approach. In [9], the effectiveness of CNN and hybrid CNN recurrent structures are studied and it can be observed that CNN based model outperforms hybrid CNN-RNN models. In [10], the authors have claimed that analyzing the traffic features from the network as a time series improves the performance of IDS. They substantiate the claim by training long short-term memory (LSTM) models with KDDCUP data set with a full and minimal feature set for 1000 epochs and have obtained a maximum accuracy of 93.82%. In [11], a scalable DL framework is proposed for intrusion detection at both the network and host levels. various ML and DNN models are trained on data sets such as KDDCUP, NSLKDD, WSN-DS, UNSW-NB15, CICIDS 2017, ADFA-LD and ADFA-WD and their performance are compared. In this work, the effectiveness of the proposed model is evaluated using standard performance metrics and it is compared with other works such as [10] and [11].

3   Data Set Description

The tcpdump data of the 1998 DARPA intrusion detection evaluation data set is pre-processed to build KDDCUP 99 data set. The feature extraction from tcpdump data is facilitated by the MADMAID data mining framework [11]. Table 1 represents the statistical information about the data set. This data set was built by capturing network traffic for ten weeks from thousands of UNIX systems and hundreds of users accessing those systems in the MIT Lincon laboratory. The data captured during the first 7 weeks were utilized for training purpose and the last 3 weeks data were utilized for testing purposes.

This data set has a total of 5 classes and 41 features. The first one is the normal class which denotes benign network traffic records. The second one is DoS. It is a kind of attack that works against resource availability. The third one is the probing attack. This class represents all attacks that are used by the attackers to obtain detailed information about the system and its security structures and configurations. This kind of attack is performed by the attacks initially in order to gain insights about the network so that they could perform many critical attacks later. The next one is R2L which denotes root to local attacks. This kind of attack is performed in order to acquire illegal remote access to any system in a network. The last one is U2R which is user to root attacks. It represents attacks that are using to gain root-level access to a system.

Table 1. Statistics of KDDCUP 99 data set

Attack types	Description	KDDCUP 99 (10% of Data)	
		Train	Test
Normal	It denotes normal traffic records	97,278	60,593
DoS	Attacker works against the resource availability	3,91,458	2,29,853
Probe	Obtaining detailed statistics of system and network configuration details	4,107	4,166
R2L	Illegal access originated from remote computer	1,126	16,189
U2R	Obtaining root or superuser level permissions illegally on a particular system	52	228
Total		4,94,021	3,11,029

4   Statistical Measures

The proposed DCNN-IDS model is evaluated using some of the most commonly used metrics such as recall, precision, f1-score, and accuracy. The Error matrix gives an overall idea about the performance of the model and These metrics are computed using terms that can be found in the error matrix. The first one is True Positive (TP) which indicates the count of malicious traffic data points that are rightly considered as malicious by the model. The second one is False Positive (FP) which indicates the count of benign traffic data points that are wrongly considered as malicious by the model. Similarly, True Negative (TN) indicates the count of benign traffic data points that are rightly considered as benign by the model. False Negative (FN) is the final term that indicates the count of malicious traffic data points that are wrongly considered as benign by the model. Based on these four terms, we can define a number of metrics:

- **Accuracy:** This term denotes the total count of right predictions (TP and TN) made by the model over total count of all predictions.

$$Accuracy = \frac{TP + TN}{TP + FP + FN + TN} \tag{1}$$

- **Precision:** This term denotes the count of right positive results over the amount of all positive results predicted by the model.

$$Precision = \frac{TP}{TP + FP} \tag{2}$$

- **Recall:** This term points to the total count of right positive results over the total count of all samples that are relevant.

$$Recall = \frac{TP}{TP + FN} \tag{3}$$

- **F1-score:** This term represents both recall and precision by taking subcontrary mean between them.

$$F1 - score = 2 * \frac{Precision * Recall}{Precision + Recall} \tag{4}$$

5 Proposed Model

The DCNN-IDS architecture is represented by the Fig. 2 The structure of the DCNN-IDS model is shown in Table 2. The proposed architecture is composed of the following sections

- **Pre-processing of network connection records**: the symbolic data in the connection records are transformed into numeric and normalized the data using L2 normalization.
- **Feature generation**: The optimal features are extracted using the proposed CNN model. The CNN model contains the convolution 1D layer which uses a one-dimensional filter that slides over the connection record in order to form a feature map. This feature map, in turn, is passed into a max-pooling layer which facilitates the dimensionality reduction. The batch normalization process is employed between the convolution and max-pooling layer to speeds up the training process and also for performance enhancement. Dropout is

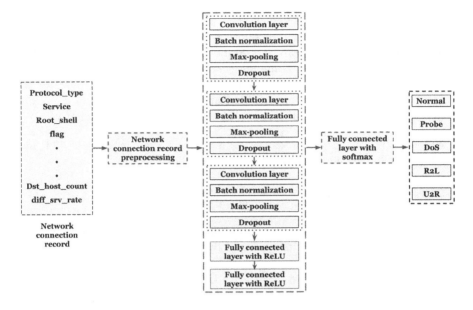

Fig. 2. Architecture of DCNN-IDS

placed after the max-pooling layer which acts as a regularization term. Since CNN has parameters, the hyperparameter tuning approach is followed to identify the optimal parameters. The value 0.01 is assigned as the learning rate and adam optimizer is utilized. The number of filters is 32 in the initial CNN layer, 64 in the next CNN layer and 128 in the final CNN layer. The parameter max-pooling length is set to 2 in all the max-pooling layers and dropout to 0.01. When the number of CNN layers increased from 3 to 4, the performance decreased and hence 3 level CNN is used. Finally, two dense layers are included along with the CNN layer and the first dense layer composed of 512 neurons and the second one is composed of 128 neurons. These layers use ReLU as the activation function.

– **Classification**: The classification is done using the fully connected layer which composed of 5 neurons with a softmax activation function.

6 Results

The proposed CNN model is designed and trained using one of the most commonly used python 3 library called Keras[1] with tensorflow[2]. The model performance is tested on the KDDCup 99 data set and the obtained results are tabulated in Table 3. The proposed CNN model outperforms than the existing LSTM [10] and DNN [11] based intrusion detection models.

---

[1] https://keras.io.

[2] https://www.tensorflow.org.

Table 2. Details about the structure proposed model

Layer type	Output shape	Parameters #
1D Convolution	(− , 41, 32)	128
Batch normalization	(− , 41, 32)	128
Max Pooling	(− , 21, 32)	−
Dropout	(− , 20, 32)	−
1D Convolution	(− , 20, 64)	6,208
Batch normalization	(− , 20, 64)	256
Max Pooling	(− , 10, 64)	−
Dropout	(− , 10, 64)	−
1D Convolution	(− , 10, 128)	24,704
Batch normalization	(− , 10, 128)	512
Max Pooling	(− , 5, 128)	−
Dropout	(− , 5, 128)	−
Flatten	(− , 640)	−
Dense	(− , 512)	3,28,192
Dropout	(− , 512)	−
Dense	(− , 128)	65,664
Dropout	(− , 128)	−
Dense	(− , 5)	645
Total parameters: 426,437		

Table 3. Evaluation of DL models on test set

Architecture	Accuracy	Precision	Recall	F1-score
LSTM [10]	93.82	82.8	58.3	68.4
DNN [11]	93.5	92	93.5	92.5
CNN (Proposed method)	**94.1**	**92.4**	**94.1**	**93**

7   Conclusion

In this paper, the effectiveness of the deep CNN model is studied for intrusion detection by modeling the network traffic data. The proposed 1D-CNN outperforms the other relevant approaches where models like DNN and LSTM are used. The proposed model uses only 425,989 parameters and does not incorporate any complicated prepossessing techniques. Therefore, it has the potential to be used in various low-powered IoT devices which has a very limited computation power. In the future, hybrid models can be used where the features are extracted from hidden layers of DL models and fed into other ML or DL models for further improvement of performance.

Acknowledgement. This work was in part supported by Paramount Computer Systems and Lakshya Cyber Security Labs. We are grateful to NVIDIA India, for the GPU hardware support to the research grant. We are also grateful to the center of Computational Engineering and Networking, Amrita School of Engineering, Amrita Vishwa Vidyapeetham, Coimbatore for encouraging the research.

References

1. Mukherjee, B., Heberlein, L.T., Levitt, K.N.: Network intrusion detection. IEEE Netw. **8**(3), 26–41 (1994)
2. Mishra, P., Varadharajan, V., Tupakula, U., Pilli, E.S.: A detailed investigation and analysis of using machine learning techniques for intrusion detection. IEEE Commun. Surv. Tutorials **21**(1), 686–728 (2018)
3. Javaid, A., Niyaz, Q., Sun, W., Alam, M.: A deep learning approach for network intrusion detection system. In Proceedings of the 9th EAI International Conference on Bio-inspired Information and Communications Technologies (formerly BIO-NETICS), pp. 21–26. ICST (Institute for Computer Sciences, Social-Informatics and Telecommunications Engineering) (2016)
4. Hodo, E., Bellekens, X., Hamilton, A., Tachtatzis, C., Atkinson, R.: Shallow and deep networks intrusion detection system: a taxonomy and survey. arXiv preprint arXiv:1701.02145 (2017)
5. Yin, C., Zhu, Y., Fei, J., He, X.: A deep learning approach for intrusion detection using recurrent neural networks. IEEE Access **5**, 21954–21961 (2017)
6. Vinayakumar, R., Soman, K.P., Poornachandran, P.: A comparative analysis of deep learning approaches for network intrusion detection systems (N-IDSs): deep learning for N-IDSs. Int. J. Digit. Crime Forensics (IJDCF) **11**(3), 65–89 (2019)
7. Vinayakumar, R., Soman, K.P., Poornachandran, P.: Evaluation of recurrent neural network and its variants for intrusion detection system (IDS). Int. J. Inf. Syst. Model. Des. (IJISMD) **8**(3), 43–63 (2017)
8. Shone, N., Ngoc, T.N., Phai, V.D., Shi, Q.: A deep learning approach to network intrusion detection. IEEE Trans. Emerg. Top. Comput. Intell. **2**(1), 41–50 (2018)
9. Vinayakumar, R., Soman, K.P., Poornachandran, P.: Applying convolutional neural network for network intrusion detection. In: 2017 International Conference on Advances in Computing, Communications and Informatics (ICACCI), pp. 1222–1228. IEEE (2017)
10. Staudemeyer, R.C.: Applying long short-term memory recurrent neural networks to intrusion detection. S. Afr. Comput. J. **56**(1), 136–154 (2015)
11. Vinayakumar, R., Alazab, M., Soman, K.P., Poornachandran, P., Al-Nemrat, A., Venkatraman, S.: Deep learning approach for intelligent intrusion detection system. IEEE Access **7**, 41525–41550 (2019)
12. Vinayakumar, R., Soman, K.P., Poornachandran, P.: Evaluating effectiveness of shallow and deep networks to intrusion detection system. In 2017 International Conference on Advances in Computing, Communications and Informatics (ICACCI), pp. 1282–1289. IEEE (2017)

Deep Learning Based Frameworks for Handling Imbalance in DGA, Email, and URL Data Analysis

K. Simran[1](✉), Prathiksha Balakrishna[2], Ravi Vinayakumar[3], and K. P. Soman[1]

[1] Center for Computational Engineering and Networking,
Amrita School of Engineering, Amrita Vishwa Vidyapeetham, Coimbatore, India
`simiketha19@gmail.com`
[2] Graduate School, Computer Science Department, Texas State University,
San Marcos, USA
`prathi.93april8@gmail.com`
[3] Center for Artificial Intelligence, Prince Mohammad Bin Fahd University,
Khobar, Saudi Arabia
`vinayakumarr77@gmail.com`

Abstract. Deep learning is a state of the art method for a lot of applications. The main issue is that most of the real-time data is highly imbalanced in nature. In order to avoid bias in training, cost-sensitive approach can be used. In this paper, we propose cost-sensitive deep learning based frameworks and the performance of the frameworks is evaluated on three different Cyber Security use cases which are Domain Generation Algorithm (DGA), Electronic mail (Email), and Uniform Resource Locator (URL). Various experiments were performed using cost-insensitive as well as cost-sensitive methods and parameters for both of these methods are set based on hyperparameter tuning. In all experiments, the cost-sensitive deep learning methods performed better than the cost-insensitive approaches. This is mainly due to the reason that cost-sensitive approach gives importance to the classes which have a very less number of samples during training and this helps to learn all the classes in a more efficient manner.

Keywords: Cyber Security · Deep learning · Cost-sensitive learning · Imbalanced data

1 Introduction

Cyber Security is an area which deals with techniques related to protecting data, programs, devices, and networks from any attack, damage, and unauthorized access [1]. There are various methods in Cyber Security to secure systems as well as networks. The classical method is a signature-based system. A signature-based system relies on regular expressions which give domain-level knowledge.

© Springer Nature Singapore Pte Ltd. 2020
S. Balusamy et al. (Eds.): ICC3 2019, CCIS 1213, pp. 93–104, 2020.
https://doi.org/10.1007/978-981-15-9700-8_8

The main issue is that these signature-based systems can identify only described malware and cannot detect novel types of attacks and even existing variant types of attacks. In order to detect "0-day" malware, the researchers have followed the application of machine learning [2].

Recently, the application of deep learning architectures are employed in Cyber Security use cases and these models can extract features implicitly whereas machine learning algorithms require manual feature engineering [3–6]. To classify DGA generated domains, different deep learning approaches were proposed in [1,7], and [2]. The real-time datasets are highly imbalanced in nature and in order to handle it properly the concept of data mining approaches can be used. In this direction, numerous amount of research is being performed. In [9], an LSTM based model is proposed to handle multiclass imbalanced data for detection of DGA botnet. In this work, the LSTM model is adapted to be cost-sensitive and performed better than other cost-insensitive approaches. The main objectives of this paper are:

1. This work proposes a cost-sensitive deep learning based framework for Cyber Security.
2. The performance of cost-sensitive approaches are evaluated on three different use cases in security namely, DGA, Email, and URL.
3. The performance of cost-sensitive models are compared with cost-insensitive models.
4. Various hyperparameter tuning methods are employed to identify the optimal network parameters and network structures.

The remaining of this paper is arranged in the following order: Sect. 2 documents a survey of the literature related to DGA, URL, and Email followed by background related to NLP, deep learning, and cost-sensitive concepts in Sect. 3. Section 4 provides a description of cyber-related tweets dataset. Section 5 describes the details of the proposed architecture. Section 6 reports the experiments, results, and observations made by the proposed architecture. Section 7 concludes the paper with remakes on future work of research.

2   Literature Survey on Deep Learning Based DGA, URL, and Email Data Analysis

2.1   Domain Generation Algorithms (DGAs)

In [8], an LSTM network was proposed for real-time prediction of DGA generated domains. This work implemented binary as well as multiclass classification of DGA. This network has a detection rate of 90% and a false positive (FP) rate of 1:10000. In [10], convolutional neural network (CNN) and LSTM deep learning models were utilized to classify large amounts of real traffic. Simple steps were followed to obtain pure DGA and non-DGA samples from real DNS traffic and achieved a false positive rate of 0.01%. In [11], deep learning based approach was proposed to classify domain name as malicious or benign. Performance of various deep learning techniques like recurrent neural network (RNN), LSTM, and classical machine learning approaches were compared. A highly scalable framework was proposed by [12] for situational awareness of Cyber Security threats. This framework analyses domain name system event data. Deep learning approaches for detection and classification of pseudo-random domain names were proposed in [13]. Comparison between different deep learning approaches like LSTM, RNN, I-RNN, CNN, and CNN-LSTM was performed. RNN and CNN-LSTM performed significantly better than other models and got a detection rate of 0.99 and 0.98 respectively. A data-driven approach was utilized in [14] to detect malware-generated domain names. This approach uses RNN and has achieved an F1-score of 0.971. A combined binary and multiclass classification model was proposed in [9] to detect DGA botnet. This model uses LSTM network and has the capability to handle imbalanced multiclass data. A comprehensive survey on detection of malicious domain using DNS data was performed by [15].

2.2 Uniform Resource Locator (URL)

A comprehensive and systematic survey to detect malicious URL using machine learning methodologies was conducted by [16]. URLNet was proposed in [17] which is an end-to-end system to detect malicious URL. This deep learning framework contains word CNNs as well as character CNNs and has the capability to learn nonlinear URL embedding directly from the URL. In [18], various deep learning frameworks such as RNN, I-RNN, LSTM, CNN, CNN-LSTM were utilized to classify real URL's into malicious and benign at the character level. LSTM and CNN-LSTM performed significantly better than other models and achieved an accuracy of 0.9996 and 0.9995 respectively. A comparative study using shallow and deep networks was performed by [19] for malicious URL's detection. In this work, CNN-LSTM network outperformed other networks by achieving an accuracy of 98%. In [20], three models namely, support vector machine (SVM) algorithm based on term frequency - inverse document frequency (TF-IDF), logistic regression algorithm and CNN based on the word2vec features were used to detect and predict malicious URLs. An online deep learning framework was proposed in [21] for detecting malicious DNS and URL. The framework utilized character-level word embedding and CNN. In this work, a real-world data set was utilized and the models performed better than state-of-art baseline methods. URLDeep was proposed in [22] to detect malicious URL's. This deep learning framework based on dynamic CNN can learn a non-linear URL address. A cost-sensitive framework firstfilter was proposed in [23] to detect malicious URL. This network can handle large-scale imbalanced network data.

2.3 Electronic Mail (Email)

A complete review for filtering of email spam was proposed in [24]. Machine learning based techniques and trends for email spam filtering were also discussed in this work. In [25], a machine learning based approach was proposed to classify email space. This framework basically classifies an email into spam and non-spam. This work also proposed a platform-independent progressive web app (PWA). In [26], deep learning based frameworks were proposed for email classification. This work proposed LSTMs and CNNs network which outperformed baseline architectures. CNN performed better than LSTM and achieved an F1 score of 84.0%. [27] proposed a multi-modal framework based on model fusion (MMA-MF) to classify email. This model fuses CNN and LSTM model. Image part of the email is processed by the CNN model whereas the text part of the email is sent to the LSTM model separately. Accuracy with a range between 92.64% to 98.48% is achieved by this method.

3 Background

This section discusses the details behind the text representation, deep learning architectures and the concept of cost-sensitive model.

3.1 Text Representation

Keras Embedding: Word embedding takes sequence and similarities into account to convert words into dense vectors of real numbers. Keras provides an embedding layer with few parameters such as dictionary size, embedding size, length of the input sequence and so on. These parameters are hyperparameters and can have an impact on the performance. The weights are taken randomly at first. These weights are tuned during backpropagation with respect to other deep learning layers. Generally, Keras embedding learns embedding of all the words or characters in the training set but the input word or character should be represented by a unique integer. Keras[1] is neural network library available for the public which has different neural network building blocks like RNN, CNN, etc. and also other common layers like dropout, pooling, etc.

N-gram: From a given sequence of text, the continuous sequences of N items are called are N-gram. N-gram with $N = 1$ is known as a unigram and it takes one word/character at once. $N = 2$ and $N = 3$ are called bigram and trigram respectively and will take two and three words/characters at a time. If n words/characters are to be taken at once then N will be equal to n.

3.2 Machine Learning

Naive Bayes: is a simple but surprisingly powerful algorithm which is based on Bayes theorem principle. Given the prior information of conditions that may be related with the occasion, it finds the probability of occurrence of an event.

---

[1] https://keras.io/.

Decision Tree: is another supervised machine learning algorithm. The decision tree is constructed by continuously splitting the data-dependent on certain parameters. Decision trees consist of leaves and nodes where leaves are the results of each decision made and nodes are the decision processes. Iterative Dichotomiser 3 (ID3) algorithm is the most commonly used algorithm to produce these trees. Using Decision Trees both classification and regression are possible for discrete and continuous data.

AdaBoost: is an ensemble machine learning classifier like random forest which utilizes a number of weak classifiers to make a strong classifier. Many machine learning algorithms performance can be boosted using AdaBoost. Training set which is used to iteratively retrain the algorithm is chosen based on the accuracy of previous training. At every iteration, there is a weight given to every trained classifier which is dependent on the accuracy achieved by the classifier. The items that were not correctly classified are given higher weights which makes them have a higher probability in next classifier. Classifier which has an accuracy of 50% or more are given zero weight whereas negative weights are given to classifier which has accuracy less the 50%. As the number of iterations is increased, the accuracy of the classifier is improved.

Random Forest (RF): At first, random forest delivers multiple decision trees. These different decision trees are then merged to get the correct classification. The accuracy of this algorithm is directly proportional to the number of decision trees. Without hyperparameter tuning, random forest gives a very good performance. To reduce overfitting, it utilizes the ensemble learning method while making the decision trees. Different types of data such as binary, numerical or categorical can be given as input to this algorithm.

Support Vector Machine (SVM): is another supervised machine learning algorithm which creates a hyperplane to split the data attributes between at least two classes. Every data attribute is projected onto an n-dimensional space. The hyperplane is created in a way such that the distance between the most nearby point of each class and the hyperplane is maximized. Hard margin SVM and soft margin SVM are the two type of SVM where hard margin SVM is the SVM which draws a hyperplane in linear manner whereas soft margin SVM is the SVM which draws the hyperplane in non-linear manner.

3.3 Deep Learning Architectures

Deep Neural Network (DNN): is an advanced model of classical feedforward network (FNN). As the name indicates the DNN contains many hidden layers along with the input and output layer. When the number of layer increases in FFN causes the vanishing and exploding gradient issue. To handle these issues, the *ReLU* non-linear activation was introduced. *ReLU* helps to protect weights from vanishing by the gradient error. Compared to other non-linear functions, *ReLU* is more robust to the first-order derivative function since it does not become zero for high positive as well as high negative values.

Convolutional Neural Network (CNN): is the most commonly used deep learning architecture in computer vision applications as it has the capability to extract spatial features. The three layers in CNN are convolution layer, pooling layer, and fully connected layer. Convolution layer contains filters that slide over the data to capture the optimal features and these features collectively are termed as a feature map. The dimension of the feature map is high and to reduce the dimension pooling layer is used. Min, max or average are the three pooling operations. Finally, the pooling features are passed into a fully connected layer for classification. For binary classification, *sigmoid* activation function is used whereas for multiclass classification, *softmax* activation function is used.

Long Short-Term Memory (LSTM): is a special type of recurrent neural network. It takes care of the issue of exploding and vanishing gradient. A cell of LSTM comprises of four major parts namely, input, state cell, three gates and output. The concatenation of the previous output and present input is the input of this LSTM cell. The focal piece of the LSTM cell is called as a state cell which holds the information about the previous sequences. The three gates in an LSTM cell are forget gate, input gate, and output gate. Which information to be remembered or which information to forget is decided by the forget gate. The information relevant to the present input is taken to the cell state by the input gate. What information should be passed as the output of the LSTM cell is decided by the output gate. The output of the present cell gets concatenated with the input of the next cell.

CNN - LSTM: CNN - LSTM architecture was developed for spatial time series prediction problems as LSTM alone cannot handle inputs with spatial structure like images. It consists of CNN layers to exact the features of the input data and LSTM for supporting sequence predictions. In the end, it is connected to a fully connected layer to get the classified output.

3.4   Cost-Sensitive Model

Models normally treat all samples equally which makes them sensitive to the class imbalance problem. Class imbalance problem arises when there are classes which have very small samples in comparison to other classes in the training data. This problem can be handled using cost-sensitive models. The cost-sensitive deep learning architectures consider all the samples equally. These models give importance to the classes that have more number of samples during training and limits the learning capability to the classes that have very less number of samples. Cost-sensitive learning served as an important method in real-world data mining applications and provides an approach to carefully handle the class imbalance problem. Let's assume that the samples have equal cost at first. $C[i,i]$ indicates the misclassification cost of the class i, which is generated using the class distribution as

$$C[i,i] = \left(\frac{1}{n_i}\right)^{\gamma} \tag{1}$$

Where $\gamma \in [0,1]$. 0 indicates that cost-sensitive deep learning architectures are diminished to cost-insensitive and 1 indicates that $C[i,i]$ is inversely proportional to the class size n_j.

4   Description of the Data Set

In this work, three different data sets were utilized for the three use cases. For DGA, domain names have to be classified as legitimate or malicious. For Email, classification result should be either legitimate or spam. For URL, URL should be classified as legitimate or malicious. The data set is divided into train data and test data. The train data set was used to train the models whereas the test data set was used to test the trained models. The train and test dataset of DGA composed of 38,276 legitimate, 53,052 malicious and 12,753 legitimate, 17,690 malicious domain name samples respectively. The legitimate domain names are collected from Alexa[2] and OpenDNS[3] and DGA generated domain names are collected from OSINT Feeds[4]. The train dataset is collected from November, 2017 to December 2017 and the test dataset is collected from January 2018 to February 2018. The train and test dataset of email composed of 19,337 legitimate, 24,665 spam and 8,153 legitimate, 10,706 email samples respectively. The train and test dataset of email are collected from Enron[5] and PU[6]. The train and test dataset of URL composed of 233,74 legitimate, 11,116 malicious and 11,42 legitimate, 578 malicious samples respectively. The legitimate URLs are collected from Alexa.com and DMOZ directory[7] and malicious URLs are collected from malwareurl.com, Phishtank.com, OpenPhish.org, malwaredomainlist.com, and malwaredomains.com. The train dataset is collected from March, 2018 to April 2018 and the test dataset is collected from September, 2018 to October, 2018. All the datasets are unique as well as the train and test datasets are disjoint to each other.

5   Proposed Architecture

The proposed architecture is shown in Fig. 1. The diagram located in top shows the training process involved in cost-insensitive deep learning model. The other

---

[2] https://support.alexa.com/hc/en-us/articles/200449834-Does-Alexa-have-a-list-of-its-top-ranked-websites.

[3] https://www.opendns.com/.

[4] https://osint.bambenekconsulting.com/feeds/.

[5] https://www.cs.cmu.edu/~enron/.

[6] http://www.aueb.gr/users/ion/data/PU123ACorpora.tar.gz.

[7] https://dmoz-odp.org/.

diagram shows the training process involved in the cost-sensitive deep learning model. In the cost-sensitive deep learning model, we introduce cost-weights to make the classifier to give importance to the classes which have very less number of samples and give less importance to the classes which have more number of samples. This enables to avoid imbalanced problems in classification.

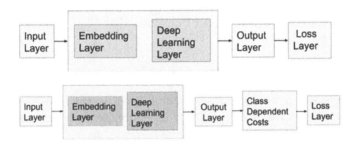

Fig. 1. Cost-insensitive and cost-sensitive deep learning based architectures.

6   Experiments, Results, and Observations

All the classical machine learning algorithms are implemented using Scikit-learn[8] and the deep learning models are implemented using TensorFlow[9] with Keras (See footnote 1) framework. All the models are trained on GPU enabled TensorFlow. Various statistical measures are utilized in order to evaluate the performance of the proposed classical machine learning and deep learning models.

We have trained various classical machine learning and deep learning model which can be cost-sensitive or cost-insensitive using the trained datasets. The performance of the trained models is evaluated on test data.

All the models are parameterized as optimal parameters play a significant role in obtaining better performance. For machine learning algorithms, we have not done any hyperparameter tuning. We have used the default parameters of Scikit-learn. To convert text into numerical values, Keras embedding was used with an embedding dimension of 128. Different architectures namely, DNN, CNN, LSTM, and CNN-LSTM are used. For DNN, 4 hidden layers with units 512, 384, 256, 128 and a finally dense layer with 1 hidden unit. In between the hidden layer dropout of 0.01 and batch normalization are used. Dropout was used to reduce overfitting and batch normalization was used to increase the speed. In CNN, 64 filters with filter length 3 and followed by maxpooling with pooling length 2 are used. Followed by a dense layer with 128 hidden units and dropout of 0.3. Finally a dense layer with one hidden unit. LSTM contains 128 memory blocks

---

[8] https://scikit-learn.org/.
[9] https://www.tensorflow.org/.

Table 1. Results for DGA analysis.

Model	Accuracy	Precision	Recall	F1-score	TN	FP	FN	TP
Naive Bayes	68.1	99.3	45.5	64.4	12,700	53	9,653	8037
Decision Tree	79.7	76.5	93.8	84.3	7,654	5,099	1091	16,599
AdaBoost	82.8	79.2	95.6	86.6	8,300	4,453	770	16,920
RF	84.1	80.5	95.8	87.5	8,651	4,102	736	16,954
SVM	85.2	81.7	96.2	88.3	8,932	3,821	680	17,010
DNN	86.8	83.7	96.1	89.5	9,434	3,319	688	17,002
CNN	94.3	92.1	98.7	95.3	11,263	1,490	233	17,457
LSTM	94.4	93.0	97.6	95.3	11,457	1,296	421	17,269
CNN-LSTM	95.2	93.2	99.0	96.0	11,478	1,275	174	15,716
Cost-sensitive models								
CNN	95.4	93.2	99.5	96.2	11,464	1,289	97	17,593
LSTM	95.5	93.2	99.6	96.3	11,470	1,283	74	17,616
CNN-LSTM	95.6	93.2	99.7	96.3	11,467	1,286	59	17,631

Table 2. Results for Email analysis.

Model	Accuracy	Precision	Recall	F1-score	TN	FP	FN	TP
Naive Bayes	68.8	99.4	45.3	62.2	8,122	31	5,855	4,851
Decision Tree	82.9	80.0	95.4	87.1	4,521	2,527	487	10,138
AdaBoost	91.3	88.6	97.1	92.7	6,815	1,338	310	10,396
RF	92.0	89.9	96.7	93.2	6,984	1,169	349	10,357
SVM	92.3	92.3	94.4	93.3	7,304	849	599	10,107
DNN	93.0	90.0	98.6	94.1	6,980	1,173	145	10,561
CNN	93.6	92.6	96.4	94.5	7,326	827	382	10,324
LSTM	93.7	91.9	97.5	94.6	7,239	914	270	10,436
CNN-LSTM	94.0	92.2	97.6	94.8	7,270	883	253	10,453
Cost-sensitive models								
CNN	94.2	92.7	97.4	95.0	7,334	819	276	10,430
LSTM	94.3	92.7	97.6	95.1	7,333	820	254	10,452
CNN-LSTM	94.7	92.8	98.3	95.5	7,341	812	187	10,519

followed by dropout of 0.3 and finally dense layer with one hidden unit. In CNN-LSTM architecture, we connected CNN network with LSTM network. CNN has 64 filters with filter length 3, followed by a maxpooling layer having pooling length 2. Followed by LSTM network having 50 memory blocks and finally a dense layer with one hidden unit is added. All the experiments are run till 100 epochs with a learning rate of 0.01, and *adam* optimizer.

Table 3. Results for URL analysis.

Model	Accuracy	Precision	Recall	F1-score	TN	FP	FN	TP
Naive Bayes	45.1	37.9	98.8	54.7	205	937	7	571
Decision Tree	81.8	73.3	72.1	72.7	990	152	161	417
AdaBoost	87.1	83.8	76.3	79.9	1,057	85	137	441
RF	90.0	90.6	78.4	84.0	1,095	47	125	453
SVM	81.0	88.4	50.0	63.9	1,104	38	289	289
DNN	90.8	92.5	79.1	85.3	1,105	37	121	457
CNN	92.9	91.9	86.5	89.1	1,098	44	78	500
LSTM	93.4	97.2	82.7	89.3	1,128	14	100	478
CNN-LSTM	94.4	96.5	86.5	91.2	1,124	18	78	500
Cost-sensitive models								
CNN	93.4	96.0	83.7	89.5	1,122	20	94	484
LSTM	94.5	93.7	89.8	91.7	1,107	35	59	519
CNN-LSTM	94.7	93.1	91.0	92.0	1,103	39	52	526

The detailed performance analysis of all the models are reported in Table 1 for DGA analysis, Table 2 for Email analysis, and Table 3 for URL analysis. As shown in the tables, the performance of deep learning models is better than the machine learning models. More importantly, the performance of cost-sensitive deep learning models is better than the cost-insensitive models. This is primarily because cost-sensitive models can give certain weights to the classes which helps to reduced overfitting and underfitting during training. We can see in all the three Tables that the cost-sensitive hybrid network of CNN-LSTM performed better than the other network like CNN and LSTM.

7   Conclusion and Future Work

This paper proposes a generalized cost-sensitive deep learning model for Cyber Security use cases such as DGA, Email, and URL. However, the model can be applied on other Cyber Security use cases also. The cost-sensitive hybrid model composed of CNN and LSTM can extract spatial and temporal features and can obtain better perform on any type of data sets. Implementing this model in real time data analysis with Big data and Streaming can be considered a good direction for future work.

Acknowledgements. This research was supported in part by Paramount Computer Systems and Lakhshya Cyber Security Labs. We are grateful to NVIDIA India, for the GPU hardware support to research grant. We are also grateful to Computational Engineering and Networking (CEN) department for encouraging the research.

References

1. Mahdavifar, S., Ghorbani, A.A.: Application of deep learning to cybersecurity: a survey. Neurocomputing **347**, 149–176 (2019)
2. Apruzzese, G., Colajanni, M., Ferretti, L., Guido, A., Marchetti, M.: On the effectiveness of machine and deep learning for cyber security. In 2018 10th International Conference on Cyber Conflict (CyCon), pp. 371–390. IEEE (2018)
3. Vinayakumar, R., Alazab, M., Soman, K.P., Poornachandran, P., Al-Nemrat, A., Venkatraman, S.: Deep learning approach for intelligent intrusion detection system. IEEE Access **7**, 41525–41550 (2019)
4. Vinayakumar, R., Soman, K. P., Poornachandran, P., Menon, P.: A deep-dive on machine learning for cybersecurity use cases. In: Machine Learning for Computer and Cyber Security: Principle, Algorithms, and Practices. CRC Press (2019)
5. Vinayakumar, R., Soman, K.P.: DeepMalNet: evaluating shallow and deep networks for static PE malware detection. ICT Express **4**(4), 255–258 (2018)
6. Vinayakumar, R., Soman, K.P., Poornachandran, P.: A comparative analysis of deep learning approaches for network intrusion detection systems (N-IDSs): deep learning for N-IDSs. Int. J. Digit. Crime Forensics (IJDCF) **11**(3), 65–89 (2019)
7. Berman, D.S., Buczak, A.L., Chavis, J.S., Corbett, C.L.: A survey of deep learning methods for cyber security. Information **10**(4), 122 (2019)
8. Woodbridge, J., Anderson, H.S., Ahuja, A., Grant, D.: Predicting domain generation algorithms with long short-term memory networks. arXiv preprint arXiv:1611.00791 (2016)
9. Tran, D., Mac, H., Tong, V., Tran, H.A., Nguyen, L.G.: A LSTM based framework for handling multiclass imbalance in DGA botnet detection. Neurocomputing **275**, 2401–2413 (2018)
10. Yu, B., Gray, D.L., Pan, J., De Cock, M., Nascimento, A.C.: Inline DGA detection with deep networks. In 2017 IEEE International Conference on Data Mining Workshops (ICDMW), pp. 683–692. IEEE (2017)
11. Vinayakumar, R., Soman, K.P., Poornachandran, P.: Detecting malicious domain names using deep learning approaches at scale. J. Intell. Fuzzy Syst. **34**(3), 1355–1367 (2018)
12. Vinayakumar, R., Poornachandran, P., Soman, K.P.: Scalable framework for cyber threat situational awareness based on domain name systems data analysis. In: Roy, S.S., Samui, P., Deo, R., Ntalampiras, S. (eds.) Big Data in Engineering Applications. SBD, vol. 44, pp. 113–142. Springer, Singapore (2018). https://doi.org/10.1007/978-981-10-8476-8_6
13. Vinayakumar, R., Soman, K.P., Poornachandran, P., Sachin Kumar, S.: Evaluating deep learning approaches to characterize and classify the DGAs at scale. J. Intell. Fuzzy Syst. **34**(3), 1265–1276 (2018)
14. Lison, P., Mavroeidis, V.: Automatic detection of malware-generated domains with recurrent neural models. arXiv preprint arXiv:1709.07102 (2017)
15. Zhauniarovich, Y., Khalil, I., Yu, T., Dacier, M.: A survey on malicious domains detection through DNS data analysis. ACM Comput. Surv. (CSUR) **51**(4), 67 (2018)
16. Sahoo, D., Liu, C., Hoi, S.C.: Malicious URL detection using machine learning: a survey. arXiv preprint arXiv:1701.07179 (2017)
17. Le, H., Pham, Q., Sahoo, D., Hoi, S.C.: URLnet: learning a URL representation with deep learning for malicious URL detection. arXiv preprint arXiv:1802.03162 (2018)

18. Vinayakumar, R., Soman, K.P., Poornachandran, P.: Evaluating deep learning approaches to characterize and classify malicious URL's. J. Intell. Fuzzy Syst. **34**(3), 1333–1343 (2018)
19. Vazhayil, A., Vinayakumar, R., Soman, K.P.: Comparative Study of the detection of malicious URLs using shallow and deep networks. In 2018 9th International Conference on Computing, Communication and Networking Technologies (ICCCNT), pp. 1–6. IEEE (2018)
20. Abdi, F.D., Wenjuan, L.: Malicious URL detection using convolutional neural network. J. Comput. Sci. Eng. Inf. Technol. 7(6), 1–8 (2017)
21. Jiang, J., et al.: A deep learning based online malicious URL and DNS detection scheme. In: Lin, X., Ghorbani, A., Ren, K., Zhu, S., Zhang, A. (eds.) SecureComm 2017. LNICST, vol. 238, pp. 438–448. Springer, Cham (2018). https://doi.org/10. 1007/978-3-319-78813-5_22
22. Wanda, P., Jie, H.J.: URLDeep: continuous prediction of malicious URL with dynamic deep learning in social networks. IJ Netw. Secur. **21**(6), 971–978 (2019)
23. Vu, L., Nguyen, P., Turaga, D.: Firstfilter: a cost-sensitive approach to malicious URL detection in large-scale enterprise networks. IBM J. Res. Dev. **60**(4), 4:1–4:10 (2016)
24. Bhowmick, A., Hazarika, S.M.: Machine learning for e-mail spam filtering: review, techniques and trends. arXiv preprint arXiv:1606.01042 (2016)
25. Alurkar, A.A., et al.: A proposed data science approach for email spam classification using machine learning techniques. In: 2017 Internet of Things Business Models, Users, and Networks, pp. 1–5. IEEE (2017)
26. Eugene, L., Caswell, I.: Making a manageable email experience with deep learning (2017)
27. Yang, H., Liu, Q., Zhou, S., Luo, Y.: A spam filtering method based on multi-modal fusion. Appl. Sci. **9**(6), 1152 (2019)

Computational Models

An *M/M/1* Queueing Model Subject to Differentiated Working Vacation and Customer Impatience

K. V. Vijayashree[(⊠)] and K. Ambika

Department of Mathematics, Anna University, Chennai, India
vkviji@annauniv.edu, ambisavi.ambika@gmail.com

Abstract. This paper deals with the stationary and transient analysis of a single server queueing model subject to differentiated working vacation and customer impatience. Customers are assumed to arrive according to a Poisson process and the service times are assumed to be exponentially distributed. When the system empties, the single server takes a vacation of some random duration (Type I) and upon his return if the system is still empty, he takes another vacation of shorter duration (Type II). Both the vacation duration are assumed to follow exponential distribution. Further, the impatient behaviour of the waiting customer due to slow service during the period of vacation is also considered. Explicit expressions for the time dependent system size probabilities are obtained in terms of confluent hyper geometric series and modified Bessel's function of first kind using Laplace transform, continued fractions and generating function methodologies. Numerical illustrations are added to depict the effect of variations in different parameter values on the time dependent probabilities.

Keywords: *M/M/1* queue · Differentiated working vacation · Customer impatience · Continued fractions · Generating functions · Confluent hypergeometric functions

1 Introduction

A vacation queueing system that distinguishes between two kinds of vacation that a server can take, namely, a shorter duration and a longer duration vacation is termed as queues subject to differentiated vacation. Ibe and Isijola (2014) obtained the analytical expressions for the steady-state system size probabilities of the *M/M/1* queueing model subject to differentiated vacation. Phung Duc (2015) considered the same model introduced by Ibe and Isijola (2014) to derive the expressions for the sojourn time and the queue length and subsequently extended the model with working vacations to obtain steady-state results for system size probabilities and certain other performance measures. Vijayashree and Janani (2018) extended the studies of Ibe and Isijola (2014) on steady-state system size probabilities of the queueing model to the corresponding time dependent analysis using the probability generating function and Laplace transforms. Customer's impatience is another important aspect of queueing models and it may occur

© Springer Nature Singapore Pte Ltd. 2020
S. Balusamy et al. (Eds.): ICC3 2019, CCIS 1213, pp. 107–122, 2020.
https://doi.org/10.1007/978-981-15-9700-8_9

due to the long wait in the queue. Recently, Suranga Sampth and Liu (2018) derived the transient solution for an *M/M/1* queue with impatient customers, differentiated vacations and a waiting server. In many practical situations, it is reasonable to assume an alternate server during the vacation duration who works at a relatively slower pace. In this context, this paper studies an *M/M/1* multiple vacation queueing models with two kinds of differentiated working vacations considering the impatient behaviour of the waiting customer during the vacation period of the server. Explicit expressions for the steady state and time-dependent system size probabilities are obtained. The model under consideration is relevant in several human involved systems like a clerk in a bank, a cashier in the super market and many more.

In recent years, the available bandwidth in communication system needs to meet several services such as video conferencing, video gaming, data off loading etc. thereby resulting in higher energy consumption. Hence, there arises a need to save the energy being consumed. With the advent of increase in mobile usage, various energy saving strategies were introduced. The IEEE.802.16e defines a sleep mode operation for conserving the power of mobile terminals. Sleep mode plays a central role for energy efficient usage in recent mobile technologies such as WiFi, 3G and WiMax. The sleep mode is characterized by the non-availability of the Mobile Stations (MS) as observed by the serving Base Stations (BS) to downlink and uplink traffic. In the data transfer between MS and BS, the MS can be modelled as a single server which in normal state is in active mode and switches off to sleep mode (Type I) and continues in listen interval (Type II) when no data packets are waiting in the buffer. In the IEEE standard the sleep state is peer specific and has two different modes of operations - light sleep and deep sleep mode. Chakraborthy (2016) revealed that there exists interesting performance tradeoffs among light sleep mode and deep sleep mode that can be explored to design an efficient power profile for mesh networks. Certain theoretical analysis work was carried out by various authors are Seo et al. (2014), Xiao (2005), Niu et al. (2001) to study the sleep mode operation employed in IEEE 802.16e. Among them, Xiao (2005) and Niu et al. (2001) construct queueing models with multiple vacations to analyse the power consumption and the delay.

2   Model Description

Consider a single server queueing model in which arrivals are allowed to join the system according to a Poisson process with parameter λ and service takes place according to an exponential distribution with parameter μ. The server takes a vacation of some random duration (type 1) if there are no customers in the system. When the server finds an empty system upon his return, the server takes another vacation of shorter duration (type 2). It is assumed that the server continues to provide service even during the vacation period, but at a slower rate rather than completely stopping the service. Such an assumption agrees well with most of the real time situations. The service time during type I and type II vacation are assumed to be exponentially distributed with parameters $\mu_1(< \mu)$ and $\mu_2(< \mu)$ respectively. Customers arriving while the system is in vacation state become impatient due to slow service. Each customer, upon arrival, activates an individual timer, which is exponentially distributed with parameter ξ for both vacation types (type I and type II). If the customer's service has not been completed before the customer's timer expires, he abandons the system never to return. It is assumed that the inter-arrival times, service times, waiting times and vacation times are mutually independent and the service discipline is First-In First-Out. Furthermore, the vacation times of the server during type I and type II vacation are also assumed to follow exponential distribution with parameters γ_1 and γ_2 respectively. The state transition diagram for the queueing model under study is given in Fig. 1.

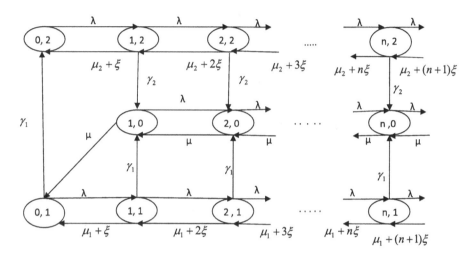

Fig. 1. State Transition Diagram of an *M/M/1* queueing system subject to differentiated working vacation and customer impatience.

Let $X(t)$ denote the number of the customer in the system and $S(t)$ represent the state of the server at time t, where $S(t) = \begin{cases} 0, & \text{if the server is busy} \\ 1, & \text{if the server is in type I vacation} \\ 2, & \text{if the server is in type II vacation.} \end{cases}$

It can be readily seen that the process $\{X(t), S(t)\}$ forms a Markov process on the state space

$$\Omega = \{(0, 1) \cup (0, 2) \cup (n, j); n = 1, 2..; j = 0, 1, 2\}.$$

2.1 Governing Equations

Let $P_{n,j}(t)$ denote the time dependent probability for the system to be in state j with n customers at time t. Assume that initially the system is empty and the server is in type I vacation. By standard methods, the system of Kolmogorov differential difference equations governing the process are given by

$$P'_{1,0}(t) = -(\lambda + \mu)P_{1,0}(t) + \mu P_{2,0}(t) + \gamma_1 P_{1,1}(t) + \gamma_2 P_{1,2}(t) \qquad (2.1)$$

$$P'_{n,0}(t) = -(\lambda + \mu)P_{n,0}(t) + \mu P_{n+1,0}(t) + \lambda P_{n-1,0}(t) + \gamma_1 P_{n,1}(t) + \gamma_2 P_{n,2}(t),$$
$$n = 2, 3..$$
$$(2.2)$$

$$P'_{0,1}(t) = -(\lambda + \gamma_1)P_{0,1}(t) + \mu P_{1,0}(t) + (\mu_1 + \xi)P_{1,1}(t) \qquad (2.3)$$

$$P'_{n,1}(t) = -(\lambda + \gamma_1 + \mu_1 + n\xi)P_{n,1}(t) + \lambda P_{n-1,1}(t) + (\mu_1 + (n+1)\xi)P_{n+1,1}(t)$$
$$(2.4)$$

$$P'_{0,2}(t) = -\lambda P_{0,2}(t) + (\mu_2 + \xi)P_{1,2}(t) + \gamma_1 P_{0,1}(t) \qquad (2.5)$$

$$P'_{n,2}(t) = -(\lambda + \gamma_2 + \mu_2 + n\xi)P_{n,2}(t) + \lambda P_{n-1,2}(t) + (\mu_2 + (n+1)\xi)P_{n+1,2}(t)$$
$$(2.6)$$

with $P_{0,1}(0) = 1$, $P_{0,2}(0) = 0$ and $P_{n,j}(0) = 0$ for $n = 1,2,3...$ and $j = 0,1,2,..$

3 Transient Analysis

In this section, the time–dependent system size probabilities for the model under consideration are obtained using Laplace transform, continued fractions and probability generating function method in terms of modified Bessel functions of first kind and confluent hypergeometric function.

3.1 Evaluation of $P_{n,1}(t)$ and $P_{n,2}(t)$

Let $\hat{P}_{n,j}(s)$ be the Laplace transform of $P_{n,j}(t)$; $n = 0, 1 \ldots$ and $j = 0, 1, 2$. Taking Laplace transform of the Eqs. (2.4) and (2.6) leads to

$$s\hat{P}_{n,1}(s) - P_{n,1}(0) = -(\lambda + \gamma_1 + \mu_1 + n\xi)\hat{P}_{n,1}(s) + \lambda \hat{P}_{n-1,1}(s)$$
$$+ (\mu_1 + (n+1)\xi)\hat{P}_{n+1,1}(s) \qquad (3.1)$$

and

$$s\hat{P}_{n,2}(s) - P_{n,2}(0) = -(\lambda + \gamma_2 + \mu_2 + n\xi)\hat{P}_{n,2}(s) + \lambda \hat{P}_{n-1,2}(s)$$
$$+ (\mu_2 + (n+1)\xi)\hat{P}_{n+1,2}(s) \qquad (3.2)$$

Using the boundary conditions and rewriting Eq. (3.1) yields

$$\frac{\hat{P}_{n,1}(s)}{\hat{P}_{n-1,1}(s)} = \frac{\lambda}{s + \lambda + \gamma_1 + \mu_1 + n\xi - (\mu_1 + (n+1)\xi)\frac{\hat{P}_{n+1,1}(s)}{\hat{P}_{n,1}(s)}}$$

which further yields the continued fraction given by

$$\frac{\hat{P}_{n,1}(s)}{\hat{P}_{n-1,1}(s)} = \cfrac{\lambda}{(s + \lambda + \gamma_1 + \mu_1 + n\xi) - \cfrac{\lambda(\mu_1 + (n+1)\xi)}{(s+\lambda+\gamma_1+\mu_1+(n+1)\xi) - \cfrac{\lambda(\mu_1+(n+2)\xi)}{(s+\lambda+\gamma_1+\mu_1+(n+2)\xi) - \cdots}}}$$

Using the identity (Refer Lorentzen and Waadeland 1992) relating continued fractions and hypergeometric series given by

$$\frac{{}_1F_1(a+1;c+1;z)}{{}_1F_1(a;c;z)} = \frac{c}{c-z} + \frac{(a+1)z}{c-z+1} \frac{(a+2)z}{c-z+2} \cdots,$$

where ${}_1F_1(a;c;z)$ is the confluent hypergeometric function, we get

$$\frac{\hat{P}_{n,1}(s)}{\hat{P}_{n-1,1}(s)} = \frac{\lambda}{\xi\left(\frac{s+\gamma_1+\mu_1}{\xi}+n\right)} \frac{{}_1F_1\left(\frac{\mu_1}{\xi}+n+1; \frac{s+\gamma_1+\mu_1}{\xi}+n+1; -\frac{\lambda}{\xi}\right)}{{}_1F_1\left(\frac{\mu_1}{\xi}+n; \frac{s+\gamma_1+\mu_1}{\xi}+n; -\frac{\lambda}{\xi}\right)},$$

for $n = 1, 2, 3 \ldots$. Hence, we recursively obtain

$$\hat{P}_{n,1}(s) = \hat{\phi}_n(s)\hat{P}_{0,1}(s) \tag{3.3}$$

where

$$\hat{\phi}_n(s) = \left(\frac{\lambda}{\xi}\right)^n \frac{1}{\prod_{i=1}^n\left(\frac{s+\gamma_1+\mu_1}{\xi}+i\right)} \frac{{}_1F_1\left(\frac{\mu_1}{\xi}+n+1; \frac{s+\gamma_1+\mu_1}{\xi}+n+1; -\frac{\lambda}{\xi}\right)}{{}_1F_1\left(\frac{\mu_1}{\xi}+1; \frac{s+\gamma_1+\mu_1}{\xi}+1; -\frac{\lambda}{\xi}\right)}.$$

In particular, when $n = 1$, Eq. (3.3) becomes

$$\hat{P}_{1,1}(s) = \hat{\phi}_1(s)\hat{P}_{0,1}(s). \tag{3.4}$$

Now, taking Laplace transform of Eq. (2.3) and applying the boundary conditions leads to

$$s\hat{P}_{0,1}(s) - P_{0,1}(0) = -(\lambda+\gamma_1)\hat{P}_{0,1}(s) + \mu\hat{P}_{1,0}(s) + (\mu_1+\xi)\hat{P}_{1,1}(s),$$

and hence

$$\hat{P}_{0,1}(s) = \frac{1}{s+\lambda+\gamma_1} + \frac{\mu}{s+\lambda+\gamma_1}\hat{P}_{1,0}(s) + \frac{(\mu_1+\xi)}{s+\lambda+\gamma_1}\hat{P}_{1,1}(s). \tag{3.5}$$

Substituting Eq. (3.4) in the Eq. (3.5) and after some algebra, we get

$$\hat{P}_{0,1}(s) = \left(1 + \mu\hat{P}_{1,0}(s)\right) \sum_{r=0}^{\infty} \frac{(\mu_1+\xi)^r\left[\hat{\phi}_1(s)\right]^r}{(s+\lambda+\gamma_1)^{r+1}}. \tag{3.6}$$

Substituting Eq. (3.6) in Eq. (3.3) yields

$$\hat{P}_{n,1}(s) = \left(1 + \mu\hat{P}_{1,0}(s)\right)\hat{\phi}_n(s) \sum_{r=0}^{\infty} \frac{(\mu_1+\xi)^r\left[\hat{\phi}_1(s)\right]^r}{(s+\lambda+\gamma_1)^{r+1}}, n = 1, 2, 3. \tag{3.7}$$

Applying the boundary conditions to Eq. (3.2) and using the same procedure as above to evaluate $\hat{P}_{n,1}(s)$, it is seen that $\hat{P}_{n,2}(s)$ can be expressed as

$$\hat{P}_{n,2}(s) = \hat{\psi}_n(s)\hat{P}_{0,2}(s) \tag{3.8}$$

where

$$\hat{\psi}_n(s) = \left(\frac{\lambda}{\xi}\right)^n \left(\frac{1}{\prod_{i=1}^n \left(\frac{s+\gamma_2+\mu_2}{\xi}+i\right)}\right) \left(\frac{{}_1F_1\left(\frac{\mu_2}{\xi}+n+1;\ \frac{s+\gamma_2+\mu_2}{\xi}+n+1;\ -\frac{\lambda}{\xi}\right)}{{}_1F_1\left(\frac{\mu_2}{\xi}+1;\ \frac{s+\gamma_2+\mu_2}{\xi}+1;\ -\frac{\lambda}{\xi}\right)}\right).$$

In particular, when $n = 1$, Eq. (3.8) becomes

$$\hat{P}_{1,2}(s) = \hat{\psi}_1(s)\hat{P}_{0,2}(s). \tag{3.9}$$

Again taking Laplace transform of Eq. (2.5) leads to

$$s\hat{P}_{0,2}(s) - P_{0,2}(0) = -\lambda\hat{P}_{0,2}(s) + (\mu_2+\xi)\hat{P}_{1,2}(s) + \gamma_1\hat{P}_{0,1}(s),$$

and hence

$$\hat{P}_{0,2}(s) = \frac{(\mu_2+\xi)}{s+\lambda}\hat{P}_{1,2}(s) + \frac{\gamma_1}{s+\lambda}\hat{P}_{0,1}(s). \tag{3.10}$$

Substituting Eq. (3.6) and Eq. (3.9) in the Eq. (3.10) and after some algebra, we get

$$\hat{P}_{0,2}(s) = \gamma_1\left(1+\mu\hat{P}_{1,0}(s)\right)\sum_{r=0}^{\infty}\frac{(\mu_1+\xi)^r\left[\hat{\phi}_1(s)\right]^r}{(s+\lambda+\gamma_1)^{r+1}}\sum_{m=0}^{\infty}\frac{(\mu_2+\xi)^m\left[\hat{\psi}_1(s)\right]^m}{(s+\lambda)^{m+1}}. \tag{3.11}$$

Substituting Eq. (3.11) in Eq. (3.8) yields

$$\hat{P}_{n,2}(s) = \gamma_1\left(1+\mu\hat{P}_{1,0}(s)\right)\hat{\psi}_n(s)\sum_{r=0}^{\infty}\frac{(\mu_1+\xi)^r\left[\hat{\phi}_1(s)\right]^r}{(s+\lambda+\gamma_1)^{r+1}}\sum_{m=0}^{\infty}\frac{(\mu_2+\xi)^m\left[\hat{\psi}_1(s)\right]^m}{(s+\lambda)^{m+1}}$$

$$\tag{3.12}$$

Taking Laplace inverse for Eq. (3.7) and Eq. (3.12) leads to

$$P_{n,1}(t) = \left(\delta(t)+\mu P_{1,0}(t)\right)*\phi_n(t)*\sum_{r=0}^{\infty}(\mu_1+\xi)^r[\phi_1(t)]^{*r}*e^{-(\lambda+\gamma_1)t}\frac{(t)^r}{r!},$$

$$n = 0, 1, 2, \ldots \tag{3.13}$$

and

$$P_{n,2}(t) = \gamma_1\left(\delta(t)+\mu P_{1,0}(t)\right)*\psi_n(t)*\sum_{r=0}^{\infty}[\phi_1(t)]^{*r}$$

$$*e^{-(\lambda+\gamma_1)t}\frac{((\mu_1+\xi)t)^r}{r!}\sum_{m=0}^{\infty}[\psi_1(t)]^{*m}*e^{-\lambda t}\frac{((\mu_2+\xi)t)^m}{m!},$$

$$n = 0, 1, 2\ldots. \tag{3.14}$$

ltiple vacation queueing systems with

where $\delta(t)$ is the Kronecker delta function and $\phi_n(t)$ and $\psi_n(t)$ for all values of n are derived in the Appendix. Therefore, all the time dependent probabilities of the number in the system during the vacation period of the server (both type I and type II vacation) are expressed in terms of $P_{1,0}(t)$. It still remains to determine $P_{1,0}(t)$.

3.2 Evaluation of $P_{n,0}(t)$

Towards this end, define the probability generating function, $Q(z, t)$ as $Q(z, t) = \sum_{n=1}^{\infty} P_{n,0}(t)z^n$. Then, $\frac{\partial Q(z,t)}{\partial t} = \sum_{n=1}^{\infty} P'_{n,0}(t)z^n$.
Multiplying Eq. (2.2) by z^n and summing it over all possible values of n leads to

$$\sum_{n=2}^{\infty} P'_{n,0}(t)z^n = -(\lambda + \mu) \sum_{n=2}^{\infty} P_{n,0}(t)z^n + \lambda z \sum_{n=2}^{\infty} P_{n-1,0}(t)z^{n-1} + \frac{\mu}{z} \sum_{n=2}^{\infty} P_{n+1,0}(t)z^{n+1}$$

$$+ \gamma_1 \sum_{n=2}^{\infty} P_{n,1}(t)z^n + \gamma_2 \sum_{n=2}^{\infty} P_{n,2}(t)z^n + (\lambda + \mu)P_{1,0}(t)z. \tag{3.15}$$

Multiplying Eq. (2.1) by z, we get

$$P'_{1,0}(t)z = -(\lambda + \mu)P_{1,0}(t)z + \mu P_{2,0}(t)z + \gamma_1 P_{1,1}(t)z + \gamma_2 P_{1,2}(t)z. \tag{3.16}$$

Now, adding the above two equations yields

$$\frac{\partial Q(z, t)}{\partial t} - \left(-(\lambda + \mu) + \frac{\mu}{z} + \lambda z\right)Q(z, t)$$

$$= \gamma_1 \sum_{n=1}^{\infty} P_{n,1}(t)z^n + \gamma_2 \sum_{n=1}^{\infty} P_{n,2}(t)z^n - \mu P_{1,0}(t).$$

Integrating the above linear differential equation with respect to 't' leads to

$$Q(z, t) = \gamma_1 \int_0^t \left(\sum_{n=1}^{\infty} P_{n,1}(y)z^n\right) e^{-(\lambda+\mu)(t-y)} e^{\left(\frac{\mu}{z}+\lambda z\right)(t-y)} dy$$

$$+ \gamma_2 \int_0^t \left(\sum_{n=1}^{\infty} P_{n,2}(y)z^n\right) e^{-(\lambda+\mu)(t-y)} e^{\left(\frac{\mu}{z}+\lambda z\right)(t-y)} dy. \tag{3.17}$$

$$- \mu \int_0^t P_{1,0}(y) e^{-(\lambda+\mu)(t-y)} e^{\left(\frac{\mu}{z}+\lambda z\right)(t-y)} dy.$$

It is well known that if $\alpha = 2\sqrt{\lambda\mu}$ and $\beta = \sqrt{\frac{\lambda}{\mu}}$, then the generating function of the modified Bessel function of the first kind of order n represented by $I_n(.)$ is given by

$$exp\left(\frac{\mu t}{z} + \lambda z t\right) = \sum_{n=-\infty}^{\infty} (\beta z)^n I_n(\alpha t).$$

Comparing the coefficients of z^n in Eq. (3.17) for $n = 1, 2, 3 \ldots$ leads to

$$P_{n,0}(t) = \gamma_1 \int_0^t \sum_{k=1}^{\infty} P_{k,1}(y)\beta^{n-k} I_{n-k}(\alpha(t - y)) e^{-(\lambda+\mu)(t-y)} dy$$

$$+ \gamma_2 \int_0^t \sum_{k=1}^{\infty} P_{k,2}(y)\beta^{n-k} I_{n-k}(\alpha(t - y)) e^{-(\lambda+\mu)(t-y)} dy$$

$$- \mu \int_0^t P_{1,0}(y) \beta^n I_n(\alpha(t-y)) e^{-(\lambda+\mu)(t-y)} dy. \tag{3.18}$$

Comparing the coefficients of z^{-n} in Eq. (3.17) yields

$$0 = \gamma_1 \int_0^t \sum_{k=1}^{\infty} P_{k,1}(y) \beta^{-n-k} I_{-n-k}(\alpha(t-y)) e^{-(\lambda+\mu)(t-y)} dy$$

$$+ \gamma_2 \int_0^t \sum_{k=1}^{\infty} P_{k,2}(y) \beta^{-n-k} I_{-n-k}(\alpha(t-y)) e^{-(\lambda+\mu)(t-y)} dy$$

$$- \mu \int_0^t P_{1,0}(y) \beta^{-n} I_{-n}(\alpha(t-y)) e^{-(\lambda+\mu)(t-y)} dy.$$

Multiplying the above equation by β^{2n} and using the property $I_{-n}(t) = I_n(t)$, we get

$$0 = \gamma_1 \int_0^t \sum_{k=1}^{\infty} P_{k,1}(y) \beta^{n-k} I_{n+k}(\alpha(t-y)) e^{-(\lambda+\mu)(t-y)} dy$$

$$+ \gamma_2 \int_0^t \sum_{k=1}^{\infty} P_{k,2}(y) \beta^{n-k} I_{n+k}(\alpha(t-y)) e^{-(\lambda+\mu)(t-y)} dy$$

$$- \mu \int_0^t P_{1,0}(y) \beta^n I_n(\alpha(t-y)) e^{-(\lambda+\mu)(t-y)} dy. \tag{3.19}$$

Subtracting Eq. (3.18) from Eq. (3.19) leads to

$$P_{n,0}(t) = \gamma_1 \int_0^t \sum_{k=1}^{\infty} P_{k,1}(y) \beta^{n-k} (I_{n-k}(\alpha(t-y)) - I_{n+k}(\alpha(t-y))) e^{-(\lambda+\mu)(t-y)} dy$$

$$+ \gamma_2 \int_0^t \sum_{k=1}^{\infty} P_{k,2}(y) \beta^{n-k} (I_{n-k}(\alpha(t-y))$$

$$- I_{n+k}(\alpha(t-y))) e^{-(\lambda+\mu)(t-y)} dy. \tag{3.20}$$

for $n = 1, 2, 3, \ldots$. Thus $P_{n,0}(t)$ is expressed in terms of $P_{k,1}(t)$ and $P_{k,2}(t)$ which are expressed in terms of $P_{1,0}(t)$ in Eq. (3.13) and Eq. (3.14) respectively. It still remains to determine $P_{1,0}(t)$ explicitly. Substituting $n = 1$ in Eq. (3.20) yields

$$P_{1,0}(t) = \gamma_1 \int_0^t \sum_{k=1}^{\infty} P_{k,1}(y) \beta^{1-k} (I_{1-k}(\alpha(t-y)) - I_{1+k}(\alpha(t-y))) e^{-(\lambda+\mu)(t-y)} dy$$

$$+ \gamma_2 \int_0^t \sum_{k=1}^{\infty} P_{k,2}(y) \beta^{1-k} (I_{1-k}(\alpha(t-y))$$

$$- I_{1+k}(\alpha(t-y))) e^{-(\lambda+\mu)(t-y)} dy.$$

Using the property $I_{k-1}(t) - I_{k+1}(t) = \frac{2k I_k(t)}{t}$ and $I_{1-k}(t) = I_{k-1}(t)$, we get

$$P_{1,0}(t) = \gamma_1 \int_0^t \sum_{k=1}^{\infty} P_{k,1}(y) \beta^{1-k} \frac{2k I_k(\alpha(t-y))}{\alpha(t-y)} e^{-(\lambda+\mu)(t-y)} dy$$

$$+ \gamma_2 \int_0^t \sum_{k=1}^{\infty} P_{k,2}(y) \beta^{1-k} \frac{2kI_k(\alpha(t-y))}{\alpha(t-y)} e^{-(\lambda+\mu)(t-y)} dy. \qquad (3.21)$$

Taking Laplace transform of Eq. (3.21) leads to

$$\hat{P}_{1,0}(s) = 2\gamma_1 \sum_{k=1}^{\infty} \hat{P}_{k,1}(s) \beta^{1-k} \frac{1}{\alpha^{-k+1} \left(p + \sqrt{p^2 - \alpha^2}\right)^k}$$

$$+ 2\gamma_2 \sum_{k=1}^{\infty} \hat{P}_{k,2}(s) \beta^{1-k} \frac{1}{\alpha^{-k+1} \left(p + \sqrt{p^2 - \alpha^2}\right)^k} \qquad (3.22)$$

where $p = s + \lambda + \mu$. Substituting for $\hat{P}_{k,1}(s)$ and $\hat{P}_{k,2}(s)$ from Eq. (3.7) and Eq. (3.12) in Eq. (3.22) leads to

$$\hat{P}_{1,0}(s) = 2\gamma_1 \sum_{k=1}^{\infty} \beta^{1-k} \frac{\left(1 + \mu \hat{P}_{1,0}(s)\right)}{\alpha^{-k+1} \left(p + \sqrt{p^2 - \alpha^2}\right)^k} \hat{\phi}_k(s) \sum_{r=0}^{\infty} \frac{(\mu_1 + \xi)^r \left[\hat{\phi}_1(s)\right]^r}{(s + \lambda + \gamma_1)^{r+1}}$$

$$+ 2\gamma_2\gamma_1 \sum_{k=1}^{\infty} \beta^{1-k} \frac{\left(1 + \mu \hat{P}_{1,0}(s)\right)}{\alpha^{-k+1} \left(p + \sqrt{p^2 - \alpha^2}\right)^k} \hat{\psi}_k(s) \sum_{r=0}^{\infty} \frac{(\mu_1 + \xi)^r \left[\hat{\phi}_1(s)\right]^r}{(s + \lambda + \gamma_1)^{r+1}}$$

$$\sum_{m=0}^{\infty} \frac{(\mu_2 + \xi)^m \left[\hat{\psi}_1(s)\right]^m}{(s + \lambda)^{m+1}},$$

which further yields

$$\hat{P}_{1,0}(s) \left(1 - \hat{H}(s)\right) = \frac{\hat{H}(s)}{\mu},$$

where

$$\hat{H}(s) = \gamma_1 \sum_{k=1}^{\infty} \left(\frac{1}{\beta}\right)^k \left(\frac{p - \sqrt{p^2 - \alpha^2}}{\alpha}\right)^k \sum_{r=0}^{\infty} \frac{(\mu_1 + \xi)^r \left[\hat{\phi}_1(s)\right]^r}{(s + \lambda + \gamma_1)^{r+1}}$$

$$\left(\hat{\phi}_k(s) + \gamma_2 \hat{\psi}_k(s) \sum_{m=0}^{\infty} \frac{(\mu_2 + \xi)^m \left[\hat{\psi}_1(s)\right]^m}{(s + \lambda)^{m+1}}\right).$$

Therefore, we get

$$\hat{P}_{1,0}(s) = \frac{\hat{H}(s)}{\mu\left(1 - \hat{H}(s)\right)} = \frac{\hat{H}(s)}{\mu} \sum_{k=0}^{\infty} \left(\hat{H}(s)\right)^k = \frac{1}{\mu} \sum_{k=0}^{\infty} \left(\hat{H}(s)\right)^{k+1}$$

Laplace inversion of the above equation yields

$$P_{1,0}(t) = \frac{1}{\mu} \sum_{k=0}^{\infty} (H(t))^{*(k+1)}, \tag{3.23}$$

where $H(t)$ is given by

$$H(t) = \gamma_1 \sum_{k=1}^{\infty} \left(\frac{1}{\beta}\right)^k \frac{k I_k(\alpha t)}{t} e^{-(\lambda+\mu)t} * \sum_{r=0}^{\infty} (\mu_1 + \xi)^r [\phi_1(t)]^{*r} * e^{-(\lambda+\gamma_1)t} \frac{(t)^r}{r!}$$

$$* \left(\phi_k(t) + \gamma_2 \psi_k(t) * \sum_{m=0}^{\infty} [\psi_1(t)]^{*m} * e^{-\lambda t} \frac{((\mu_2 + \xi)t)^m}{m!}\right)$$

Note that Eqs. (3.13) and (3.14) present explicit expressions for $P_{n,1}(t)$ and $P_{n,2}(t)$ in terms of $P_{1,0}(t)$ where $P_{1,0}(t)$ is given by Eq. (3.23). All other probabilities, namely $P_{n,0}(t)$ are determined in terms of $P_{n,1}(t)$ and $P_{n,2}(t)$ in Eq. (3.20). Therefore, all the time –dependent probabilities are explicitly obtained in terms of modified Bessel function of the first kind using generating function methodology. Having determined the transient state probabilities, all other performance measures can be readily analysed.

4 Steady State Probabilities

Let $\pi_{n,j}$ denote the steady – state probability for the system to be in state j with n customers. Mathematically,

$$\pi_{n,j} = \lim_{t \to \infty} P_{n,j}(t)$$

Using the final value theorem of Laplace transform, which states

$$\lim_{t \to \infty} P_{n,j}(t) = \lim_{s \to 0} s \hat{P}_{n,j}(s).$$

It is observed that

$$\pi_{n,j} = \lim_{s \to 0} s \hat{P}_{n,j}(s),$$

From Eq. (3.17), we get

$$\lim_{s \to 0} s \hat{P}_{n,1}(s) = \lim_{s \to 0} s \left\{ \left(1 + \mu \hat{P}_{1,0}(s)\right) \hat{\phi}_n(s) \sum_{r=0}^{\infty} \frac{(\mu_1 + \xi)^r [\hat{\phi}_1(s)]^r}{(s + \lambda + \gamma_1)^{r+1}} \right\},$$

and hence

$$\pi_{n,1} = \left[\mu \phi_n \sum_{r=0}^{\infty} \frac{(\mu_1 + \xi)^r [\phi_1]^r}{(\lambda + \gamma_1)^{r+1}} \right] \pi_{1,0}.$$

where

$$\phi_n = \lim_{s\to 0} s\hat{\phi}_n(s) = \left(\frac{\lambda}{\xi}\right)^n \frac{1}{\prod_{i=1}^{n}\left(\frac{\gamma_1+\mu_1}{\xi}+i\right)} \frac{{}_1F_1\left(\frac{\mu_1}{\xi}+n+1;\,\frac{\gamma_1+\mu_1}{\xi}+n+1;\,-\frac{\lambda}{\xi}\right)}{{}_1F_1\left(\frac{\mu_1}{\xi}+1;\,\frac{\gamma_1+\mu_1}{\xi}+1;\,-\frac{\lambda}{\xi}\right)}.$$

Similarly, from Eq. (3.10), we get

$$\lim_{s\to 0} s\hat{P}_{n,2}(s) = \lim_{s\to 0} s\left\{ \gamma_1\left(1+\mu\hat{P}_{1,0}(s)\right)\hat{\psi}_n(s) \sum_{r=0}^{\infty} \frac{(\mu_1+\xi)^r\left[\hat{\phi}_1(s)\right]^r}{(s+\lambda+\gamma_1)^{r+1}} \right.$$

$$\left. \sum_{m=0}^{\infty} \frac{(\mu_2+\xi)^m\left[\hat{\psi}_1(s)\right]^m}{(s+\lambda)^{m+1}} \right\}$$

and hence

$$\pi_{n,2} = \left[\gamma_1\mu\psi_n \sum_{r=0}^{\infty} \frac{(\mu_1+\xi)^r[\phi_1]^r}{(\lambda+\gamma_1)^{r+1}} \sum_{m=0}^{\infty} \frac{(\mu_2+\xi)^m[\psi_1]^m}{(\lambda)^{m+1}} \right]\pi_{1,0}.$$

where

$$\psi_n = \lim_{s\to 0} s\hat{\psi}_n(s) = \left(\frac{\lambda}{\xi}\right)^n \frac{1}{\prod_{i=1}^{n}\left(\frac{\gamma_2+\mu_2}{\xi}+i\right)} \frac{{}_1F_1\left(\frac{\mu_2}{\xi}+n+1;\,\frac{\gamma_2+\mu_2}{\xi}+n+1;\,-\frac{\lambda}{\xi}\right)}{{}_1F_1\left(\frac{\mu_2}{\xi}+1;\,\frac{\gamma_2+\mu_2}{\xi}+1;\,-\frac{\lambda}{\xi}\right)}.$$

Also, consider the Laplace transform of Eq. (3.20) given by

$$\hat{P}_{n,0}(s) = \sum_{n=1}^{\infty}\left\{ \gamma_1 \sum_{k=1}^{\infty} \hat{P}_{k,1}(s)\beta^{n-k} \left\{ \frac{\left(p-\sqrt{p^2-\alpha^2}\right)^{n-k}}{\alpha^{n-k}\sqrt{p^2-\alpha^2}} - \frac{\left(p-\sqrt{p^2-\alpha^2}\right)^{n+k}}{\alpha^{n+k}\sqrt{p^2-\alpha^2}} \right\} \right.$$

$$\left. + \gamma_2 \sum_{k=1}^{\infty} \hat{P}_{k,2}(s)\beta^{n-k} \left\{ \frac{\left(p-\sqrt{p^2-\alpha^2}\right)^{n-k}}{\alpha^{n-k}\sqrt{p^2-\alpha^2}} - \frac{\left(p-\sqrt{p^2-\alpha^2}\right)^{n+k}}{\alpha^{n+k}\sqrt{p^2-\alpha^2}} \right\} \right\},$$

where $p = s+\lambda+\mu$. It is seen that

$$\lim_{s\to 0} s\hat{P}_{n,0}(s) = \gamma_1 \sum_{k=1}^{\infty} \pi_{k,1}\beta^{n-k} \frac{1}{\lambda-\mu}\left\{ \left(\frac{2\mu}{\alpha}\right)^{n-k} - \left(\frac{2\mu}{\alpha}\right)^{n+k} \right\}$$

$$+ \gamma_2 \sum_{k=1}^{\infty} \pi_{k,2}\beta^{n-k} \frac{1}{\lambda-\mu}\left\{ \left(\frac{2\mu}{\alpha}\right)^{n-k} - \left(\frac{2\mu}{\alpha}\right)^{n+k} \right\}.$$

On simplification, we get

$$\pi_{n,0} = \frac{1}{\lambda-\mu}\left\{ \sum_{k=1}^{\infty} [\gamma_1\pi_{k,1}+\gamma_2\pi_{k,2}]\left(1-\left(\frac{\mu}{\lambda}\right)^k\right) \right\},$$

which reduces to

$$
\pi_{n,0} = \frac{\pi_{1,0}}{\lambda - \mu} \left\{ \sum_{k=1}^{\infty} \left[\gamma_1 \left(\mu \phi_k \sum_{r=0}^{\infty} \frac{(\mu_1 + \xi)^r [\phi_1]^r}{(\lambda + \gamma_1)^{r+1}} \right) \right. \right.
$$
$$
\left. \left. + \gamma_2 \left(\gamma_1 \mu \psi_k \sum_{r=0}^{\infty} \frac{(\mu_1 + \xi)^r [\phi_1]^r}{(\lambda + \gamma_1)^{r+1}} \sum_{m=0}^{\infty} \frac{(\mu_2 + \xi)^m [\psi_1]^m}{(\lambda)^{m+1}} \right) \right] \left(1 - \left(\frac{\mu}{\lambda} \right)^k \right) \right\},
$$

Therefore,

$$
\pi_{n,0} = \frac{\gamma_1 \mu}{\lambda - \mu} \left\{ \sum_{k=1}^{\infty} \left[\sum_{r=0}^{\infty} \frac{(\mu_1 + \xi)^r [\phi_1]^r}{(\lambda + \gamma_1)^{i+1}} \left[\phi_k + \gamma_2 \psi_k \sum_{m=0}^{\infty} \frac{(\mu_2 + \xi)^m [\psi_1]^m}{(\lambda)^{m+1}} \right] \right] \right.
$$
$$
\left. \left(1 - \left(\frac{\mu}{\lambda} \right)^k \right) \right\} \pi_{1,0}.
$$

As a special case, when $\mu_1 = 0 = \mu_2$ and $\xi = 0$ the results are seen to coincide with Vijayashree and Janani (2018).

5 Numerical Illustrations

This section illustrates the behaviour of time-dependent state probabilities of the system during the functional state and vacation states (type 1 and type 2) of the server against time for appropriate choice of the parameter values. Though the system is of infinite capacity, the value of n is restricted to 25 for the purpose of numerical study.

Figure 2 depicts the behaviour of $P_{n,0}(t)$ against time for varying values of n with the values $\lambda = 0.4$, $\mu = 0.6$, $\gamma_1 = 0.8$, $\gamma_2 = 1$, $\mu_1 = 0.1$, $\mu_2 = 0.05$ and $\xi = 0.01$. It is seen that for a particular value of n the transient state probability increases as time progresses and converges to the corresponding steady state probabilities. However, for a particular value of t the value of the probability decreases with increase in the number of customer in the system.

Figure 3 and Fig. 4 depicts the variation of $P_{n,1}(t)$ and $P_{n,2}(t)$ against time t for varying values of n with the same parameter values. All the values of $P_{n,1}(t)$ and $P_{n,2}(t)$ are start at 0 and converges to the corresponding to the steady state probability . It is observed that for a particular instant of time the probability values decreases as n increases. However, for a particular value of n the probability values increases reaches a peak and gradually decreases till it converges.

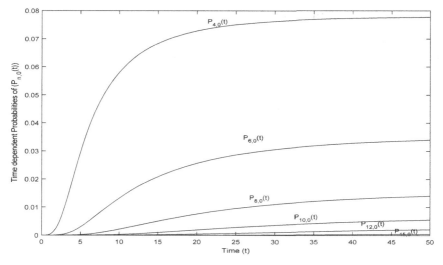

Fig. 2. Behaviour of $P_{n,0}(t)$ against t for varying values of n.

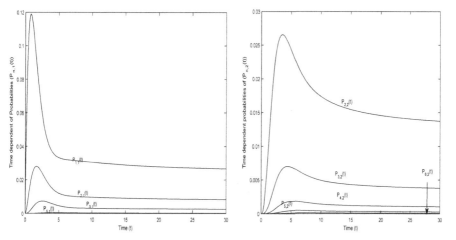

Fig. 3. Behaviour of $P_{n,1}(t)$
against t for varying values of n.

Fig. 4. Behaviour of $P_{n,2}(t)$
against t for varying values of n.

6 Conclusions

This paper presents a time dependent analysis of an *M/M/1* queueing model subject to differentiated working vacation and customer impatience. Closed form expressions for the transient state probabilities of the state of the system are obtained using generating function and continued fraction methodologies. Numerical illustrations are added to support the theoretical results. The study can be further extended to an *M/M/1* queueing model subject to m kinds of differentiated working vacation with impatience.

Appendix: Derivation of $\phi_n(t)$ and $\psi_n(t)$

The confluent hypergeometric function represented by $_1F_1(a; c; z)$ has a series representation given by

$$_1F_1(a; c; z) = 1 + \frac{a}{c}\frac{z}{1!} + \frac{a}{c}\frac{a(a+1)}{(c+1)}\frac{z^2}{2!} + \ldots = 1 + \sum_{k=1}^{\infty} \frac{\prod_{j=1}^{k-1}(a+i)}{\prod_{i=0}^{k-1}(c+i)} \frac{z^k}{k!}$$

Consider the repression for $\hat{\phi}_n(s)$ obtained as

$$\hat{\phi}_n(s) = \left(\frac{\lambda}{\xi}\right)^n \frac{1}{\prod_{i=1}^{n}\left(\frac{s+\gamma_1+\mu_1}{\xi}+i\right)} \frac{_1F_1\left(\frac{\mu_1}{\xi}+n+1; \frac{s+\gamma_1+\mu_1}{\xi}+n+1; -\frac{\lambda}{\xi}\right)}{_1F_1\left(\frac{\mu_1}{\xi}+1; \frac{s+\gamma_1+\mu_1}{\xi}+1; -\frac{\lambda}{\xi}\right)}. \quad (A.1)$$

Using the definition of confluent hypergeometric function, we obtain

$$_1F_1\left(\frac{\mu_1}{\xi}+n+1; \frac{s+\gamma_1+\mu_1}{\xi}+n+1; -\frac{\lambda}{\xi}\right) = \sum_{k=0}^{\infty} \frac{\prod_{j=1}^{k}(\mu_1+(n+j)\xi)}{\prod_{i=1}^{n+k}(s+\gamma_1+\mu_1+i\xi)} \frac{(-\lambda)^k}{\xi^{k-n}k!}$$

And hence

$$\frac{_1F_1\left(\frac{\mu_1}{\xi}+n+1; \frac{s+\gamma_1+\mu_1}{\xi}+n+1; -\frac{\lambda}{\xi}\right)}{\prod_{i=1}^{n}\left(\frac{s+\gamma_1+\mu_1}{\xi}+i\right)} = \sum_{k=0}^{\infty} \frac{\prod_{j=1}^{k}(\mu_1+(n+j)\xi)}{\prod_{i=1}^{n+k}(s+\gamma_1+\mu_1+i\xi)} \frac{(-\lambda)^k}{\xi^{k-n}k!}$$

Applying partial fraction in the above equation, we get

$$\frac{_1F_1\left(\frac{\mu_1}{\xi}+n+1; \frac{s+\gamma_1+\mu_1}{\xi}+n+1; -\frac{\lambda}{\xi}\right)}{\prod_{i=1}^{n}\left(\frac{s+\gamma_1+\mu_1}{\xi}+i\right)} = \sum_{k=0}^{\infty} \frac{\prod_{j=1}^{k}(\mu_1+(n+j)\xi)}{k!} \frac{(-\lambda)^k}{\xi^{2k-1}}$$

$$\sum_{i=1}^{n+k}\left(\frac{(-1)^{i-1}}{(i-1)!(n+k-i)!}\right)\left(\frac{1}{s+\gamma_1+\mu_1+i\xi}\right) \quad (A.2)$$

Now, consider the term in the denominator of $\hat{\phi}_n(s)$ as

$$_1F_1\left(\frac{\mu_1}{\xi}+1; \frac{s+\gamma_1+\mu_1}{\xi}+1; -\frac{\lambda}{\xi}\right) = \sum_{k=0}^{\infty} \frac{\prod_{j=1}^{k}(\mu_1+j\xi)}{\prod_{i=1}^{k}(s+\gamma_1+\mu_1+i\xi)} \frac{(-\lambda)^k}{\xi^k k!}$$

$$= \sum_{k=0}^{\infty}(-\lambda)^k \hat{a}_k(s)$$

Where $\hat{a}_k(s) = \frac{\prod_{j=1}^{k}(\mu_1+j\xi)}{\prod_{i=1}^{k}(s+\gamma_1+\mu_1+i\xi)}\left(\frac{1}{\xi^k k!}\right)$ and $\hat{a}_0(s) = 1$. By resolving into partial fractions, we have

$$\hat{a}_k(s) = \frac{1}{\xi^{2k-1}k!}\sum_{r=1}^{k} \frac{\prod_{j=1}^{k}(\mu_1+j\xi)(-1)^{r-1}}{(r-1)!(k-r)!} \frac{1}{s+\gamma_1+\mu_1+r\xi}, \text{ for } k = 1, 2, 3\ldots$$

Using the identity is given by Gradshteyn et al. (2007), it is seen that

$$\left[{}_1F_1\left(\frac{\mu_1}{\xi}+1; \frac{s+\gamma_1+\mu_1}{\xi}+1; -\frac{\lambda}{\xi}\right)\right]^{-1} = \left[\sum_{k=0}^{\infty} \hat{a}_k(s)(-\lambda)^k\right]^{-1} = \sum_{k=0}^{\infty} \hat{b}_k(s)\lambda^k$$

(A.3)

where $\hat{b}_0(s) = 1$ and for $k = 1, 2, 3 \ldots$

$$\hat{b}_k(s) = \begin{vmatrix} \hat{a}_1(s) & 1 & & \cdots \\ \hat{a}_2(s) & \hat{a}_1(s) & 1 & \cdots \\ \hat{a}_3(s) & \hat{a}_2(s) & \hat{a}_2(s) & \cdots \\ & \cdots & & \cdots & \cdots & \cdots \\ \hat{a}_{k-1}(s) & \hat{a}_{k-2}(s) & \hat{a}_{k-3}(s) & \cdots & \hat{a}_1(s) & 1 \\ \hat{a}_k(s) & \hat{a}_{k-1}(s) & \hat{a}_{k-2}(s) & \cdots & \hat{a}_2(s) & \hat{a}_1(s) \end{vmatrix}$$

$$= \sum_{i=1}^{k}(-1)^{i-1}\hat{a}_i(s)\hat{b}_{k-i}(s).$$

Substituting Eq. (A.3) and Eq. (A.2) in Eq. (A.1), we get

$$\hat{\phi}_n(s) = \lambda^n\xi^n \sum_{k=0}^{\infty}(-\lambda)^k \frac{\prod_{j=1}^{k}(\mu_1 + (n+j)\xi)}{\prod_{j=1}^{k}(\mu_1 + j\xi)}\hat{a}_{n+k}(s) \sum_{j=1}^{\infty}\lambda^j\hat{b}_j(s).$$

Taking inverse Laplace transform of the above equation leads to

$$\phi_n(t) = \lambda^n\xi^n \sum_{k=0}^{\infty}(-\lambda)^k \frac{\prod_{j=1}^{k}(\mu_1 + (n+j)\xi)}{\prod_{j=1}^{k}(\mu_1 + j\xi)}a_{n+k}(t) * \sum_{j=1}^{\infty}\lambda^j b_j(t),$$

where

$$a_k(t) = \frac{1}{\xi^{2k-1}k!} \sum_{r=1}^{k} \frac{\prod_{j=1}^{k}(\mu_1 + j\xi)(-1)^{r-1}}{(r-1)!(k-r)!}e^{-(\gamma_1+\mu_1+r\xi)t}, k = 1, 2, \ldots$$

and

$$b_k(t) = \sum_{i=1}^{k}(-1)^{i-1}a_i(t) * b_{k-i}(t), k = 2, 3, \ldots, b_1(t) = a_1(t)$$

Similarly equation of $\hat{\psi}_n(s)$ as

$$\hat{\psi}_n(s) = \lambda^n\xi^n \sum_{k=0}^{\infty}(-\lambda)^k \frac{\prod_{j=1}^{k}(\mu_2 + (n+j)\xi)}{\prod_{j=1}^{k}(\mu_2 + j\xi)}\hat{c}_{n+k}(s) \sum_{j=1}^{\infty}\lambda^j\hat{d}_j(s).$$

Proceeding in the similar manner as that of $\hat{\phi}_n(s)$, it is seen that the Laplace inverse of $\hat{\psi}_n(s)$ is

$$\psi_n(t) = \lambda^n \xi^n \sum_{k=0}^{\infty} (-\lambda)^k \frac{\prod_{j=1}^{k}(\mu_2 + (n+j)\xi)}{\prod_{j=1}^{k}(\mu_2 + j\xi)} c_{n+k}(t) * \sum_{j=1}^{j} \lambda^j d_j(t).$$

where

$$c_k(t) = \frac{1}{\xi^{2k-1}k!} \sum_{r=1}^{k} \frac{\prod_{j=1}^{k}(\mu_2 + j\xi)(-1)^k}{(r-1)!(k-r)!} e^{-(\gamma_2 + \mu_2 + r\xi)t}, k = 1, 2, \ldots$$

and

$$d_k(t) = \sum_{i=1}^{k} (-1)^{i-1} c_i(t) * d_{k-i}(t), k = 2, 3, \ldots$$

References

Gradshteyn, I., Ryzhik, I., Jeffery, A., Zwillinger, D. (eds.): Table of Integrals, Series and Products, 7th edn. Academic Press, Elsevier (2007)

Ibe, O.C., Isijola, O.A.: *M/M/1* multiple vacation queueing systems with differentiated vacation. Model. Simul. Eng. **6**, 1–6 (2014)

Seo, J.-B., Lee, S.-Q., Park, N.-H., Lee, H.-W., Cho, C.-H. (eds.): Performance analysis of sleep mode operation in IEEE 802.16e. In: 38th IEEE Vehicular Technology Conference, vol. 2, pp. 1169–1173 (2004)

Lorentzen, L., Waadeland, H.: Continued Fractions with Applications. Studies in Computational Mathematics, vol. 3. Elsevier, Amsterdam (1992)

Chakrabory, S.: Analyzing peer specific power saving in IEEE 802.11s through queueing petri Nnets: some insights and future research directions. IEEE Trans. Wireless Commun. **15**, 3746–3754 (2016)

Suranga Sampth, M.I.G., Liu, J.: Impact of customer Impatience on an *M/M/1* queueing system subject to differentiated vacations with a waiting server. Qual. Tech. Quant. Manag. (2018). https://doi.org/10.1080/16843703.2018.1555877

Phung-Duc, T.: Single-server systems with power-saving modes. In: Gribaudo, M., Manini, D., Remke, A. (eds.) ASMTA 2015. LNCS, vol. 9081, pp. 158–172. Springer, Cham (2015). https://doi.org/10.1007/978-3-319-18579-8_12

Vijayashree, K.V., Janani, B.: Transient analysis of an *M/M/1* queueing system subject to differentiated vacations. Qual. Tech. Quant. Manage. **15**, 730–748 (2018)

Xiao, Y.: Energy saving mechanism in the IEEE 80216e wireless MAN. IEEE Commun. Lett. **9**, 595–597 (2005)

Niu, Z., Zhu, Y., Benetis, V.: A phase-type based markov chain model for IEEE 802.16e sleep mode and its performance analysis. In: Proceeding of the 20th International Teletraffic Congress, Canada, pp. 17–21 (2001)

Author Index

Printed in the United States
By Bookmasters